Isaiah 58:6–9

Is not this the kind of fasting I have chosen:
to loose the chains of injustice
and untie the cords of the yoke,
to set the oppressed free
and break every yoke?

Is it not to share your food with the hungry
and to provide the poor wanderer with shelter—
when you see the naked, to clothe them,
and not to turn away from your own flesh and blood?

Then your light will break forth like the dawn,
and your healing will quickly appear;
then your righteousness will go before you,
and the glory of the Lord will be your rear guard.

Then you will call, and the Lord will answer;
you will cry for help, and he will say: Here am I.

CREATED
TO
FLOURISH

Endorsements

The present age is a truly unique historical moment. The richest people ever to walk the face of the earth coexist with billions living in conditions not fit for creatures bearing the image of almighty God. How are Christians to respond to this crisis? Drawing on their many years of experience in microfinance, Peter Greer and Phil Smith challenge readers to join God's mission of helping those in poverty to flourish through restoring them to sustainable work. This book is a timely and prophetic word, combining solid theology, best practices, and deeply moving stories from the front lines.

Brian Fikkert, PhD, Founder and President, The Chalmers Center, and Coauthor, *When Helping Hurts: How to Alleviate Poverty without Hurting the Poor ... and Yourself*

Created to Flourish is an honest, insightful, and practical resource forged from the vast experience of the authors who deeply care about seeing people lifted from poverty. I am grateful to have this book in my hands and know it will add wisdom to all those who have joined the revolution.

Chuck Bentley, CEO, Crown Financial Ministries

My friends Peter and Phil have written a book about respect—not pity. They have not written a book about money—but about discovering value in hidden places with explosive benefits for individuals, families, and entire countries.

Fred Smith, President, The Gathering

Most Christians recognize the biblical mandate to care for the poor. But "doing good" doesn't always really help. With biblical insight, economic savvy, realism, and loads of wisdom, Greer and Smith point to a paradigm that can empower "the least among us." This is must reading for church mission committees, development workers, and anyone who wants to truly make a difference in the face of poverty. Moreover, Greer and Smith rightly believe that physical poverty and spiritual poverty can be addressed together without losing the integrity of the other.

Dennis Hollinger, PhD, President & Colman M. Mockler
Distinguished Professor of Christian Ethics,
Gordon-Conwell Theological Seminary

It's unusual to discover an engaging, detailed, and affecting manual delineating a Christian approach to alleviating global poverty. That's what Greer and Smith have given readers in this resource-rich guide to how individuals, businesses, churches, and denominational groups can use the basics of microfinance—the provision of financial services to the poor—to partner with communities and find "employment-based solutions with proven results for effectively reducing poverty and extending the kingdom of God."

Publishers Weekly

What a needed book! In a relational, story-based way, Peter and Phil help us learn more about microfinance and other employment-based solutions to the problem of world poverty. As we see the Church awakening more than ever to issues of social justice, this book is arriving just at the right time.

Rebecca St. James, Author, Singer, Actress

Created to Flourish is a light to the path of social entrepreneurs, students, and philanthropists showing how to help the poor physically while proclaiming the Good News of Jesus. You will learn how to avoid unintentional harm and how to do the greatest good.

Chris Crane, Founder and CEO, Edify

This book illustrates integrated solutions to spiritual and physical poverty with clarity and conviction. A must-read as we critically consider biblical stewardship of our resources.

David Weekley, Businessman, Philanthropist

The authors bring profound understanding to one of the greatest challenges throughout all of time. With an understanding of cultures coupled with intellectual strength, this book singularly defines practical and successful ways ordinary people can help fight poverty around the world. This book can effect systemic change and make a lasting difference in the world by changing the way leaders think.

Peter W. Teague, EdD, President,
Lancaster Bible College & Graduate School

There has never been a time or place that has allowed followers of Christ so many opportunities to empower the materially poor. Peter Greer and Phil Smith provide a comprehensive landscape of opportunities and practical next steps—borne out of their own experience and fueled by their joy and fulfillment along the path.

Todd Engelsen, President, PEER Servants

Leading an organization that continually seeks the balance between *word* and *deed*, I greatly appreciate Peter and Phil's passion for addressing both physical *and* spiritual needs. Christ-followers are called to love the Lord our God and our neighbor as ourselves. That means a recognition that people need bread *and* the Bread of Life, water *and* Living Water. It's a both/and, not either/or.

Kevin Palau, President, Luis Palau Association

CREATED

TO

FLOURISH

How Employment-Based Solutions Help Eradicate Poverty

PETER GREER & PHIL SMITH

EDITED BY **ERIN LONGENECKER**

FOREWORD BY **JEFF RUTT, FOUNDER OF HOPE INTERNATIONAL**

Created to Flourish

Copyright © 2016 by Peter Greer and Phil Smith

Published by HOPE International

227 Granite Run Drive, Suite 250
Lancaster, Pennsylvania 17601

www.hopeinternational.org

Cataloging-in-Publication Data

Greer, Peter, 1975–
    Created to flourish : how employment-based solutions help eradicate poverty / Peter
Greer and Phil Smith.
        p.   cm.
    Includes bibliographical references.
        ISBN 978-0-9980539-8-1 (pdf)
        ISBN 978-0-9980539-6-7 (e-book)
        ISBN 978-0-9980539-7-4 (print)
        1. Poverty—Religious aspects—Christianity. 2. Church work with the poor. I. Smith,
Philip B. (Philip Bartlett) II. Title.
    BV4647.P6G74   2016
    261.8´325—dc22   2016952470

For photography credits, see page 244.

Printed in China

TO LAUREL AND SHANNON

Previously published as The Poor Will Be Glad, *this updated book celebrates that all people are created by God to flourish. We believe God made us to employ our unique giftings and passions in service of the world around us, to engage in meaningful relationships, and to experience the dignity and joy that comes from knowing we're wonderfully made and uniquely loved by our Creator.*

God has created us to flourish.

BURUND

Contents

PART III: JOINING THE REVOLUTION

*Please visit **www.createdtoflourish.org** for an in-depth study guide on the book and for more information.*

Acronyms

APR	Annual percentage rate
ASCA	Accumulating savings and credit association
CCT	Center for Community Transformation
CGAP	Consultative Group to Assist the Poor
CMBC	Calvary Monument Bible Church
GNP	Gross national product
IFAD	International Fund for Agricultural Development
MED	Microenterprise development
MFI	Microfinance institution
NGO	Non-governmental organization
ROSCA	Rotating savings and credit association
SCA	Savings and credit association
SME	Small and medium enterprise

Foreword

(JEFF RUTT)

After the fall of the Soviet Union, Ukraine faced a debilitating economic crisis, leaving many without enough food to eat or clothes to wear. Along with others in my church, I felt compelled to respond. There were people who were hungry, who needed shelter, who didn't have the hope of Jesus Christ. As we read in Isaiah 58:7, God has a specific idea about how we should translate our faith into action:

> Is it not to share your food with the hungry
> and to provide the poor wanderer with shelter—
>
> when you see the naked, to clothe them,
> and not to turn away from your own flesh and blood?   *Isaiah 58:7*

We couldn't turn away, so my church in Lancaster, Pennsylvania, established a partnership with Pastor Leonid Petrenko and his church in Zaporozhye, a city located along the Dnieper River in southeastern Ukraine. We wanted to respond not just with money or donations but through building relationships. We greatly desired to join together as communities of faith seeking mutual encouragement.

Eager to respond to pressing needs, we began transporting containers of flour, rice, canned meat, clothing, and medical supplies. It seemed like a way we could care for the physical needs of our global neighbors, following Jesus' command that if you have two tunics, you should give one away.

Before long, distributing the donated food and supplies to the people of his church and community had become a regular part of Pastor Petrenko's job.

But as we visited the community over the next three years, we began to question our approach. Was all that free flour we were shipping proving more harmful to local flour vendors than the country's economic crisis? Were we causing businesses to suffer, or even fail? After all, why would people pay for flour when they could get it for free?

On one of our trips, over dinner with Pastor Petrenko and his family at their home, we started discussing the aid containers. He shared that people, himself included, were grateful for the generosity of our church, and that he wasn't sure what they would have done without our help. But then Pastor Petrenko, never one to mince words, asked a question that would change the course of my life: "Isn't there a way you can help us help ourselves?"

In that simple question, he had articulated the doubts and questions that had been growing in my mind and heart for a while: Was our church's approach sustainable? We were providing for physical needs, but in the meantime, we were hurting local businesses, and we weren't really breaking through the poverty. As Michael Fairbanks, cofounder of the SEVEN Fund, puts it, we had responded out of a heart for those living in poverty, but we had yet to develop a mind for them.[1]

Was there another way?

Following that eye-opening visit to Ukraine, I spent months praying, researching, and even attempting some new approaches. Eventually, I started reading about something called "microfinance." At the time, this was a little-known strategy for alleviating poverty that involved making small loans to people who had little access to credit but had the vision to begin or expand a business.

This was a breakthrough moment: Microfinance seemed to offer a way to put more power and dignity into the hands of the people in Zaporozhye, investing in their dreams and ideas rather than just offering traditional charity.

While there was much I didn't know about this approach, I believed God was calling me to step out in faith. After much prayer and seeking the counsel of those around me, HOPE International was registered as a 501(c)(3) nonprofit organization in May 1997, and the next year, HOPE officially disbursed its first loans to entrepreneurs in Zaporozhye.

In the years since then, God has grown HOPE in ways I could not have imagined. Since its founding, HOPE has become a global ministry, supporting microfinance institutions and church-based savings and credit associations across countries in Africa, Asia, Eastern Europe, and Latin America.

With its unique emphasis on Christ-centeredness, HOPE has developed an approach to poverty alleviation that seeks to address not only material poverty but also personal, relational, and spiritual brokenness.

As just one example of the power of this approach, Janviere Kamana is a widow supporting five children and three grandchildren in Burundi through her flour business. Janviere heard about a savings group through the local church and began saving $3 a week. With a $100 loan from her group, Janviere bought a bulk order of cassava, a staple root crop, to grind into flour. With her increased profits, she purchased a plot of land, where she was building a home for her family. Janviere also experienced the blessing of fellowship and friendship as she learned, prayed, and celebrated with her savings group.

I started my journey giving away flour, but today I find even greater joy seeing entrepreneurs like Janviere equipped to provide flour for their own communities.

In this book, Peter and Phil share how entrepreneurship is a pathway out of poverty. Instead of offering handouts, they provide a roadmap to help you invest in dreams, inviting people to use their God-given gifts, abilities, and resources to provide for their families and draw near to Christ.

Created to Flourish reveals the Christ-centered heart and mind I hope inspires you to love God and your neighbors around the world.

—Jeff Rutt, Founder & Board Chair of HOPE International, Founder & CEO of Keystone Custom Homes

Glimpses of Poverty

We cannot hide from the problem of poverty—it is everywhere. We may cross the street to avoid a homeless man, but that moves us closer to a TV in a storefront window where the eyes of a desperate child in a relief agency's commercial beg us: Do something! Stopping to consider poverty is uncomfortable—it makes us feel guilty. What can one person really do about such an enormous problem or even about one homeless person? It's easy to keep walking and pretend we don't see.

A growing movement is opening our eyes to the reality of poverty around the world. Bono is singing and advocating for the vulnerable in sub-Saharan Africa, while Bill and Melinda Gates are pouring massive resources into forgotten regions of the globe. Millions of Christ-followers are working to bring justice, mercy, and lasting compassion to the parts of our world most in need.

The explosion of global short-term missions is challenging the conscience of the Church in the U.S.[1] More and more of us are beginning to understand that the lifestyle we enjoy is far from universal. We are the richest of the rich—our complaints about a mall's holiday traffic jams would be baffling to our brothers and sisters in poverty around the world. Alongside this realization is the radical conviction that we need to act: Our faith must change how we live and how we respond to the needs of others—or it will be a faith that is "dead" (James 2:17).

The question before the Church in the U.S. is this: How can we transform compassion and good intentions into action that makes a lasting difference?

If we understand that Jesus wasn't simply making a polite observation when He said, "From the one who has been entrusted with much, much more will be asked" (Luke 12:48), we must ask ourselves what we are doing with our material blessings. How do we serve those in poverty? How should we?

These are critical questions. Deeply concerned about the physical and spiritual poverty in our world, we are searching for ways that followers of Christ can effectively serve. And we believe that Jesus' example and Scripture should inform our actions.

However, the answers aren't always as clear as the questions. With the publication of books like *Toxic Charity* and *When Helping Hurts*, describing the often harmful effects of helping those in need, many have come to recognize that taking effective action is not as easy as it might seem. Wise involvement in church-led international ministries could lift millions out of poverty and help build vital local churches in every corner of the globe—but these results are not inevitable simply because there is a surge of excitement or good intentions.

This book examines how followers of Christ can best counter global poverty. We explore common faults in many Christian-based anti-poverty programs and suggest employment-based solutions for effectively reducing poverty and extending the Kingdom of God. Among these solutions are savings mobilization and microfinance services, which, when paired with discipling relationships and the Gospel, provide some of the most effective methods of addressing poverty in all its dimensions.

Allow us to briefly introduce ourselves before we begin to discuss global poverty and its possible solutions.

PETER GREER

Who can forget the white Ford Bronco on every television on June 12, 1994? I was completing my freshman year of college when O. J. Simpson became *the* subject of conversation. Did you see the chase? Would the glove fit? What would Johnny Cochran say next? What I failed to realize was that another tragedy was occurring simultaneously on another continent.

Beginning in April 1994, the small central African country of Rwanda was torn apart by genocide. In only 100 days, over 800,000 people were brutally murdered in a systematic ethnic cleansing. Until the movie *Hotel Rwanda* brought this horror into many comfortable living rooms, it was rare to find someone who really knew about this tragedy.

In 1999, I moved to Rwanda with two suitcases and a desire to help. I was the managing director of Urwego, a Rwandan microfinance institution with the mission of alleviating physical and spiritual poverty through small loans and biblically based business training.[2] In Rwanda, my worldview and my Christian faith were radically reshaped. I was confronted by a level of physical need previously unimaginable to someone who grew up in a comfortable Boston suburb. I was shocked by how little I knew about the genocide and the dehumanizing effects of extreme poverty. Until then, my faith had been sheltered and safe.

How should I respond to the emotional and physical scars of a friend who managed to survive the genocide by nearly submerging herself for days in a latrine? How could I help a woman who exchanged sex for food to lovingly feed her children? What about the orphans whose parents were painfully killed by AIDS? How can those of us who have been given so much be so callous to the needs of the world? And why isn't the Church doing more to help?

Returning to the U.S. to attend graduate school at Harvard University provided an extraordinary opportunity to study macroeconomics, econometrics, and economic development and consider the question, "Why are some countries mired in poverty and volatility?" Still, some of my deepest questions remained unanswered. These were questions about how our faith should inform our service and why Jesus described His ministry as "to proclaim good news to the poor" (Luke 4:18). As a pastor's kid, I grew up hearing from missionaries who planted churches, yet I saw few models where followers of Jesus Christ met both physical and spiritual needs around the world. Scripture is emphatic about the importance of both; why did the Church often seem to neglect physical concerns?

Today, as president and CEO of HOPE International, an organization focused on Christ-centered economic development in some of the least-served areas in the world, I have the privilege of seeking answers to these vital questions. Through my travels to places ranging from small towns in Haiti to remote villages in northern Afghanistan, I have come to believe three very basic statements about global poverty and our response:

- Poverty in many parts of the world is far worse than most North Americans understand, but despite the significant depth and breadth of poverty, the situation is not hopeless.

- Employment and economic development, when partnered with discipleship, are the most effective and lasting ways of addressing physical and spiritual poverty.

- This is a critical time for the Church in the United States to fight poverty in a way that demonstrates what the Church stands *for* and not only what it stands *against*.

Everywhere I look, I see signs pointing toward a new engagement with global poverty. The Church is ready for engagement—and all we need is a clear pathway to turn our enthusiasm into actions that will radically impact poverty and bring the love of Christ to those who haven't heard. We hope this book helps fuel this rapidly growing movement.

PHIL SMITH

I'm not a preacher, a missionary, or the head of an international aid organization. However, my experience as the CEO of two large companies has given me a special perspective on creative business solutions that can be used to help people living in financial poverty.

In 2002, I began trying to understand how to spend the rest of my life doing the "good works, which God prepared in advance for [me] to do" (Ephesians 2:10). For the next five years, I involved myself in many charitable activities as I searched for the right fit for my business skills. As a part of my search, I learned about microfinance and began funding projects in countries I never knew existed—I distinctly remember the shock of discovering that Malawi is a country in Africa, not an island in Hawaii! To share what I was learning, I coauthored *A Billion Bootstraps* with Eric Thurman in 2007, a book about microfinance from a donor's perspective that also addresses the broader question of how to give effectively.

But something important was still missing—until I had a life-changing aha! moment. Aha! moments are when your heart aches, your knees quake, and your beliefs shake. They are moments of clarity when the scales fall from your eyes and you see the world in a new way. My moment happened at lunch with Mitch Wilburn, a pastor at a church in the buckle of the Bible Belt—Tulsa, Oklahoma.

Mitch told me about traveling to Haiti to visit Brad, a friend from college. Brad had been a burly, violent football player during his college years, but he'd experienced his own aha! moment and decided to become a nurse so he could help meet the physical and spiritual needs of families in Haiti, especially babies living with HIV and AIDS. Brad helped the community where he lived build a school, a medical clinic, and a church, and he developed new techniques to care for sick children.

With tears in his eyes, Mitch described watching Brad tenderly hold a tiny baby in his massive hands. It was clear this baby would soon die. Mitch asked,

"How many dying babies have you held?" Nothing could have prepared him for his crushing aha! moment that followed as Brad met his eyes and replied, "This week?"

Having lunch in that plush country club dining room with Mitch, I was shocked into clarity by Brad's story. No matter how hard I try, there is no way I can truly understand even a fraction of the problems of the world's 2.1 billion people who live on less than $3.10 a day.[3] How do the comforting words of my faith that I repeat so easily sound to people struggling to find daily food?

This powerful moment caused me to reread the New Testament several times in an effort to understand what the Bible says about helping families in poverty and sharing the Gospel with them. Easy answers and misconceptions which had long dominated my Christian beliefs began to look less and less like the ones Jesus would have in this day and time.

This book integrates practical information on global poverty with an earnest call to the Church to respond quickly, wisely, and compassionately—to be the hands and the voice of God's love. Those living in poverty have much to teach our complacent Western church. We need to understand global poverty before we can begin to work on suggestions and solutions. But first, learn how a little girl in India with a fistful of flower petals changed a father's life.

PART I

The Presence of Poverty

1

Flower Petals in the Face

(PETER)

Mumbai, the capital city of India's Maharashtra province, is known as India's financial capital and the home of Bollywood films. In a remote town 150 miles southwest of Mumbai and worlds away from the glitz and glamour of the city, Grace Orphanage provides a refuge for abandoned children. When our small group of U.S. visitors arrived, we were welcomed by a line of girls holding handfuls of flower petals. One small girl named Malika[1] emerged from the shadows of the dimly lit door frame wearing a yellow sari. Instead of gently tossing her flower petals on the ground in front of the visitors as the other girls did, her eyes sparkled as she threw them directly at us! She reminded me of my daughter—the same smile, spunk, and ineffable glow. Accompanied by the beat of Indian drums and the wail of the sitar, she danced and twirled with the other girls in a welcome ceremony.

I struggled to understand what a girl like Malika was doing in this orphanage. She should have been dancing at home with her loving parents and siblings, the way things are "supposed to be." Instead, she was one girl out of dozens at this isolated orphanage in India. What circumstances brought her here? Later that evening, we learned that several of these girls had been "indentured servants"—child slaves—and had suffered unspeakable abuse.

Their parents had seen no options other than selling off one child in order to provide food for their remaining children.

That evening as I tossed and turned beneath my mosquito net, I couldn't help comparing my daughter, Liliana, and my new friend, Malika. Both were around age 5, but they were living radically different lives. Liliana lives in her own room decorated with hanging butterflies, white bunk beds, and pastel pink bedspreads. Malika shares a drab yellow room with 24 other girls. Liliana eats three full meals a day that have incredible variety and loves Little Nemo fruit snacks in the afternoon, while Malika eats lentil porridge every day and is thankful for the special occasions when she eats meat. Liliana attends Sunday school every week without a thought for her safety. Malika lives in a country where attackers regularly vandalize Christian churches and homes, and threaten, harass, and even kill Indian Christians.[2]

INDIA

The heartbreaking reality is that these differences are largely the result of one fact: Liliana was born in the U.S., and Malika was born in India. This fact means that my daughter—and many other children born in the United States—will most likely never face certain evils and injustices that are the daily reality for hundreds of millions of children in the world.

Hunger

Liliana will never go to bed hungry unless she refuses to eat her broccoli and her parents are trying to teach her an important lesson. In developing countries, approximately 795 million people go to bed hungry every night and search for creative ways to ignore their discomfort.[3] Andrew Samuel, a banker who grew up in India, remembers his mother telling him to sleep on his stomach because it helped quell hunger pains.

Child Mortality

It is highly unlikely that Liliana will experience the pain of losing a brother or sister before she reaches adulthood. Worldwide, 5.9 million children die every year before reaching their fifth birthday. That translates to 16,000 children who die each day from hunger and preventable disease—one child every six seconds.[4]

Drinking Water

Liliana can drink directly from a faucet at one of the four sinks in our home without any concern for her health. Around the world, 663 million people don't have access to improved water sources, and nearly 2 billion may be drinking from contaminated water.[5] Millions walk long distances to carry every drop of water to their homes.

Toilets and Diarrhea

Liliana has access to indoor plumbing and considers diarrhea a temporary inconvenience. In the developing world, diarrhea wracks the bodies of millions of children who have no access to diapers or plumbing—and it kills about 530,000 children every year.[6]

Education

Liliana attends our city's public schools for free. While literacy rates have been increasing around the world, 757 million adults still lack basic reading and writing skills. Women are disproportionally represented in this number, making up two-thirds of the total.[7]

Health Care

Liliana dislikes the pain of routine shots provided by her doctor. In developing areas, only half of women receive the health care they need.[8] Over half of deaths of children under the age of 5 are from preventable or easily treatable diseases, such as pneumonia, diarrhea, and malaria.[9]

Life Expectancy

If statistical models are correct, Liliana will live past the age of 80. If she were born in Swaziland, she wouldn't expect to live much past the age of 50.[10]

Washing Machine and a Change of Clothes

Liliana's mother and I wash her clothes easily in a washing machine and choose her clothes from a dresser full of options. In other parts of the world, children—and often their mothers—must hand wash every item of clothing, a labor- and time-intensive task.

Women's Rights

My daughter will have to overcome certain biases because she is a woman. But these hurdles pale by comparison to the experience of so many others in the developing world. An Afghan man was told that his sick daughter's life could be saved if he took her across a dangerous mountain pass to medical care in a city two hours away. "No, I don't want to do that," he responded. "Girls are free, but donkeys cost money."[11]

Employment

On my way to work today, I passed at least a dozen businesses with "Help Wanted" signs, many of which would be happy to hire Liliana if she were 16. In Zimbabwe, 95 percent of the *entire population* is unemployed or underemployed.[12] There simply are no formal employment options, no "Help Wanted" signs, and no employers who are legally mandated to provide a minimum wage and other basic rights.

RWANDA

Financial Services

Liliana and I opened a savings account at our local bank branch when she turned 5. Such an account would be a luxury for the 2 billion people around the world who do not have access to financial services. Access to an account is heavily dependent on where you live, with 91 percent of adults in high-income countries having an account compared to just 28 percent in low-income countries.[13]

The reality is that the scale of poverty in the developing world dwarfs nearly everything we label as "poor" in the United States. This is exceptionally difficult for most Americans to understand, including me. Growing up, I was the "poor pastor's kid" in a wealthy Boston suburb. When everyone else had Nintendos, I had hand-me-down Ataris. How naïve I was to equate slightly less luxury with the dehumanizing struggle to survive that confronts the over 2.1 billion people who try to survive on less than $3.10 a day.[14]

Poverty in the United States is still a very real problem. Events like Hurricane Katrina remind us of just how many Americans are without an adequate safety net, not to mention daily necessities. However, the vast majority of poverty in the U.S. is "defined poverty" or "relative poverty." If "poverty" is defined as the 10 percent of the people in a nation earning the lowest income, then 10 percent of that nation will always live in poverty no matter how many resources they have. Without suggesting that their pain should be ignored, most people living in poverty in the United States have astounding resources when compared to those in the developing world.[15]

An article in *The Economist* treated this issue by comparing the lives of Dr. Mbwebwe Kabamba, a prominent surgeon in Kinshasa, the capital of the Democratic Republic of Congo, and Enos Banks, an unemployed coal driver in eastern Kentucky's Appalachia region. Both men live on nearly the same amount of money, yet there are significant differences in their lifestyles. Dr. Kabamba has no running water at his house, has the benefits from electricity twice a week, only dreams of air conditioning, and eats meat about twice a month. In the America of Enos Banks, three quarters of impoverished house-holds have air conditioning, and families in poverty eat more meat than the well-to-do. On average, those living in poverty in the U.S. are likely to live longer than those in other countries; spend more years in education; have jobs; and own cars, refrigerators, stereos, and other luxuries. The article sum-marizes: "All one can say is that whereas the poor in Kinshasa complain about the price of bread, the poor in Kentucky complain about the price of motor insurance."[16]

Let us reiterate: It is not our intention to suggest that Americans suffer no pain or hardship or that the Church should not be helping those in need in our own cities. Rather, we wish to emphasize the extreme and immediate needs of people living in poverty in developing countries. There are people who struggle to survive *every day of their lives*. The extent of this global pov-erty is staggering. According to the Pew Research Center, 71 percent of the world's population lives on less than $10 a day—the threshold considered necessary to avoid falling back into poverty:

- 949 million live on $2 or less a day.
- 3.4 billion live on $2.01 to $10 a day.[17]

The wealthy, and that includes most of us reading this book, lead lives that many consider an unreachable dream.[18]

WHAT NOW?

Ruth Callanta, founder of the Center for Community Transformation in the Philippines, wondered, "Why do we live in a place that has so much, and yet there are so many in poverty? Are there not enough fish in the sea? Does the earth not have the capacity to provide sufficient food? This cannot be what God has planned for His creation. Something is definitely wrong."[19]

Something *is* wrong. But in the haze of desperation and despair, hope is breaking through. The Church is beginning to combat extreme poverty in a new way. This movement is radically different from traditional charity. It focuses on long-term systemic change and lasting employment patterns, not short-term quick fixes. It emphasizes the importance of partnerships and local champions, not external "saviors" descending to solve the problems of those considered less fortunate. The hope of the Gospel is integrated through tangible acts of compassion that have long-term reach, rather than simply providing handouts that keep people in a position of dependency.

This is a movement where discipleship, job creation, training, and financial services are building on local relationships to empower communities to break free from poverty. It's time for a new approach to how we actively and enthusiastically think about loving our global neighbors.

2
Making a Feast for Jesus

(PHIL)

Three out of four ways the Church tries to share the Gospel will fail to have long-term results. I think Jesus implies as much in the parable of the soils (Matthew 13:3-23). So we shouldn't be surprised when money and effort spent on sharing the Good News often seem to have little long-term benefit. There are two choices: continue to do the same things over and over and expect different results (which is one definition of insanity), or imitate the example in another parable and change the way we do things. In Luke 13:6-9, Jesus describes a worker who wasn't content to have soil conditions that would result in an unproductive tree. He took the initiative to change the soil by digging and fertilizing. Isn't it time to consider modifying some of our past methods in an attempt to improve how effectively we share the Gospel with the whole world?

As we consider Gospel-sharing efforts in the developing world, we are immediately faced with an issue that cannot be ignored: How much of the Church's precious resources should be used to contend with the genuine problem of poverty?

Since Jesus said, "The poor you will always have with you" (Matthew 26:11), isn't attempting to alleviate poverty a pointless task, like pouring water down

a drain? Besides, isn't a healthy portion of the money we pay in taxes funding the massive amounts of aid the United States sends to developing countries? Wouldn't working to end poverty distract the Church from its mission of proclaiming salvation in Jesus Christ? And doesn't it seem like the Church should be focused on achievable goals rather than a utopian social dream?

My understanding of poverty and the Church's proper response began to change at home in my favorite room—the kitchen. My wife, Shannon, is a professional chef who loves teaching youngsters how to cook. Peeking into the kitchen one day, I saw my daughter and three other girls cooking. Meredith was chopping onions with sunglasses on to keep her eyes from watering, while Hanna was tentatively cutting carrots, and the two other girls were working at their own assigned tasks. Under Shannon's tutelage, these teenagers were making a feast of roasted pepper pork with raspberry sauce, garlic potatoes, and fresh sautéed green beans.

As I walked back to my office, it hit me. Meredith wasn't just mechanically chopping onions; she was making a *feast*. Hanna wasn't just cutting carrots;

she was preparing a *banquet*. With a common purpose, recipes, and team-work, the girls were creating something greater and more beautiful than the sum of its parts. While you can chop vegetables without making a feast, you can't make a feast without chopping vegetables.

Sitting in my office, I thought about the Church's stance on international poverty and missions. "What are we making?" I wondered. "A feast or just a mountain of carrot sticks?" There are Christians doing millions of tasks around the world every day. We give away wheelchairs, start orphanages, pass out bags of rice, and dig wells. We proclaim the Gospel, teach in theo-logical institutions, and plant churches.

Surely all these activities are "good," but how do they join together in making a savory feast? What is the recipe that should unite the efforts of the Church? Here is the key question—is serving those in poverty a distraction from our "core" mission of evangelism and discipleship, or is it a necessary ingredient? Jesus said, "People will come from east and west and north and south, and will take their places at the feast in the kingdom of God" (Luke 13:29). As we consider how to do our part in making the feast and increasing the number of invitees, let's explore the biblical and historical background of service to families in need and examine its contemporary relevance.

A PARADOX

For the first 50 years of my life, I didn't recognize one of the paradoxes in my thought process. Most churches I attended had a missions committee fo-cused on evangelism and a separate benevolence committee that responded to need. This structure disconnected proclaiming the Gospel from meeting physical needs. Church members seemed to internalize the message that the two functions were separate.

Missions committees were motivated and directed by Scriptures such as, "Therefore go and make disciples of all nations, baptizing them in the name of the Father and of the Son and of the Holy Spirit, and teaching them to obey everything I have commanded you" (Matthew 28:19-20); "But you will receive power when the Holy Spirit comes on you; and you will be my witnesses in Jerusalem, and in all Judea and Samaria, and to the ends of the earth" (Acts 1:8); "And how can they hear without someone preaching to them? And how can anyone preach unless they are sent? As it is written: 'How beautiful are the feet of those who bring good news!'" (Romans 10:14-15). With these Scriptures in mind, the missions committees spent their budgets primarily on sending U.S. missionaries overseas or to isolated communities in the U.S.

Benevolence committees were motivated by Scriptures such as, "Truly I tell you, whatever you did for one of the least of these brothers and sisters of mine, you did for me" (Matthew 25:40); "Sell everything you have and give to the poor, and you will have treasure in heaven" (Luke 18:22); and "Suppose a brother or a sister is without clothes and daily food. If one of you says to them, 'Go in peace; keep warm and well fed,' but does nothing about their physical needs, what good is it?" (James 2:15-16). Heeding these words, they feed the hungry, clothe the naked, and shelter the homeless. Most often this occurs in the local community, but sometimes it is done overseas too.

The acts of meeting spiritual needs and physical needs are so often separated that many Christians no longer seem to notice. The following chart is a useful gauge of your own view of the Church's mission and perhaps of the way you were raised. Where would you place yourself and your local church? Do you tend to emphasize the proclamation of the Good News of Jesus Christ or to live out your faith through acts of compassion and service?

	LOW EMPHASIS ON DEED	HIGH EMPHASIS ON DEED
LOW EMPHASIS ON WORD		
HIGH EMPHASIS ON WORD		

How does Scripture lead us in thinking through this issue? Let's examine the life of Christ and the response of the early Church.

THE EXAMPLE OF JESUS

In Luke 4:16-30, Jesus publicly declares His mandate on earth for the first time. He is speaking to people who think they know Him, yet His words produce a murderous fury. What could have been so inflammatory?

Jesus first reads from the Old Testament passage of Isaiah 61:1-2: "The Spirit of the Lord is on me, because he has anointed me to proclaim good news to the poor. He has sent me to proclaim freedom for the prisoners and recovery of sight for the blind, to set the oppressed free, to proclaim the year of the Lord's favor" (Luke 4:18-19). Jesus takes those familiar words and startles His listeners with His one-point sermon: "Today this scripture is fulfilled in your hearing" (v. 21). He goes on to say these benefits will extend to those outside of the Jewish faith.

RWANDA

When Jesus spoke of "the year of the Lord's favor," He was probably referring to the year of Jubilee. Every 50 years, a trumpet was blown on the Day of Atonement to "proclaim liberty throughout the land to all its inhabitants" (Leviticus 25:10). This proclamation freed people from crushing debt and slavery and returned land to families who had been forced by economic hardship to sell it. Jubilee alleviated the worst effects of continuing indebtedness and poverty; it was the release from debt and the restoration of rightful inheritance.

This way of describing Jesus' mission has both concrete and spiritual dimensions. The word *release* in Greek, Aramaic, and Hebrew means breaking free from financial debts as well as the release from or forgiveness of sins. God is concerned about economic realities, physical imprisonment, and visual blindness, but He also speaks of freedom from the debt of sin and spiritual bondage.

Jesus lived this full definition of release by combining care for the physical person with care for the soul. From the beginning, "Jesus went throughout Galilee, teaching in their synagogues, proclaiming the good news of the kingdom, and healing every disease and sickness among the people" (Matthew 4:23). He both proclaimed and demonstrated freedom in its most complete sense.

At the start of Jesus' ministry, John the Baptist sent two of his men to Jesus with this question: "Are you the one who is to come, or should we expect someone else?" As Luke tells the story in Luke 7:18-23, it appears Jesus heard the question and, without saying a word, turned away and continued whatever He was already doing. After a time, Jesus sent the two men back to John with instructions to tell him what they had seen and heard: "The blind receive sight, the lame walk, those who have leprosy are cleansed, the deaf hear, the dead are raised, and the good news is proclaimed to the poor" (v. 22). When Jesus specifically sets out to prove that He is the Messiah, the Promised One, what does He do? He meets physical needs *and* preaches Good News.

There were times when Jesus taught and other times He simply met people's physical needs. In each situation, He did what best demonstrated the expansive nature of the Kingdom of God—that it will last for eternity and is already here changing lives. Rather than viewing the actions and teachings of Jesus as a rainbow spectrum of loving and necessary interactions, we often separate the colors with a distorted prism because we want to emphasize one thing or another. Perhaps we have a personal preference for spoken evangelism or for fighting physical hunger, but our preferences should not place filters before our eyes and cause us to ignore the balance that's so evident in the life of Christ.

A clear example of an unfiltered viewpoint is the interplay between the Great Commission and the Greatest Commandment. Not long before departing the earth, Jesus commissioned His disciples, saying, "Therefore go and make disciples of all nations, baptizing them in the name of the Father and of the Son and of the Holy Spirit, and teaching them to obey everything I have commanded you" (Matthew 28:19-20).

Yet only a few weeks earlier, Jesus had given the Greatest Commandment by stating, "'Love the Lord your God with all your heart and with all your soul and with all your mind.' This is the first and greatest commandment. And the second is like it: 'Love your neighbor as yourself'" (Matthew 22:37-39). The ministry of Christ demonstrated the seamless harmony of obeying both the Great Commission and the Greatest Commandment.

THE EARLY DISCIPLES

Immediately following the death and resurrection of Jesus Christ, His followers imitated His pattern of meeting both physical and spiritual needs.[1] They understood the ministry of Jesus was to be continued on earth through them by the power of the Holy Spirit. The disciples did not separate doing good works from proclaiming the Good News. The Gospel wasn't only an abstract idea that could "save souls" but tangible good news with earthly relevance.

This had been impressed on the disciples not only by the daily actions of Jesus but in their first assignments.

When Jesus sent out the 12 apostles, and later when He sent out the 70 disciples, His instructions focused on two things: preaching the Good News *and* meeting physical needs. Their results were so astounding, Jesus said, "I saw Satan fall like lightning from heaven" (Luke 10:18).

Many years later, the concern of James, Peter, and John that those in poverty be included in the ongoing proclamation of Christ's message prompted them to encourage Paul to "continue to remember the poor." Paul's response was that this was "the very thing I had been eager to do all along" (Galatians 2:10). That may seem an unlikely response from the apostle so well known for his theological writings that focus on orthodoxy (right beliefs). Yet Paul was just as concerned about orthopraxis (right living) and how faith impacts the way we serve others.

For Paul, a proper understanding of what God does for us should change the way we live, including how we interact with people in poverty. Take the example of the church Paul started in Ephesus, which changed the culture of its city and swelled to as many as 50,000 members. Acts 19 shows Paul's progress and influence there. He first tried to take the Gospel to the Jews in that city. After limited success, he started the first Christian college. In just two years, Paul may have lectured more than 4,000 hours in the school, but he did more than just preach the Good News: "God did extraordinary miracles through Paul, so that even handkerchiefs and aprons that had touched him were taken to the sick, and their illnesses were cured and the evil spirits left them" (Acts 19:11-12).

In Paul's last meeting with the elders of Ephesus, he emphasized the importance of both sharing the Gospel directly and meeting physical needs. He said, "However, I consider my life worth nothing to me; my only aim is to finish the race and complete the task the Lord Jesus has given me—the task of testifying to the good news of God's grace" (Acts 20:24). He continued, "In everything I did, I showed you that by this kind of hard work we must help the weak, remembering the words the Lord Jesus himself said: 'It is more blessed to give than to receive'" (Acts 20:35).

Paul, perhaps the Church's most influential theologian, knew followers of Christ were called to an integrated life. There is no question that throughout the New Testament, the apostles and other leaders were intent on meeting both the spiritual and physical needs of others, just as Jesus was. In the following centuries, early Christians were intent on doing the same.

THE EARLY CHURCH

Rodney Stark argues persuasively in *The Rise of Christianity* that Christianity rose to prominence in the Roman world during the first three centuries after Jesus because Christians met the physical and spiritual needs of people even during times of plague and suffering.[2] He says the obscure Jewish sect became a dominant religious force as a result of its social benefits. In times

MOLDOVA

of crisis, Christians loved all people, not just "their own." The early centuries of Christianity were trying and difficult times, and epidemics were rampant. Out of fear of catching these illnesses, unbelievers often fled outbreaks, while Christians stayed behind to provide care for those in need. As a result, many unbelievers—who had been essentially abandoned by their previous social networks—converted to Christianity. The doctrines of the Christian faith suddenly made sense to people because they saw that the everyday practice of those doctrines produced a better life. Consequently, Christian community was something for which many people longed.

Christianity grew because it was attractive and inclusive. When suffering people received the love of a Christian community, they often wanted to be a part of that community. While the early Christians still longed for the rewards of heaven, they experienced the blessings of God in their day-to-day lives as well.

Due to the influence of Constantine in the fourth century CE, the Roman Catholic Church became the dominant repository of Christian life in the Western world. Its history of meeting spiritual and physical needs since then is uneven, but certainly there have been leaders of great compassion throughout the centuries, such as St. Augustine, whose church conducted rescue operations when slave ships landed in their town; St. Francis of Assisi, famous for both helping those in poverty and preaching the Gospel; and St. Catherine of Siena, who stayed behind to care for the sick when others fled the onslaught of the plague in the 14th century.

18ᵀᴴ- AND 19ᵀᴴ-CENTURY CHRISTIANS

In 18th- and 19th-century England and United States, the pattern of engagement with social concerns remained an unmistakable companion for the message of Christ. One historian said that this period, known as the Evangelical Revival, "did more to transfigure the moral character of the general populace than any other movement British history can record."[3]

The Clapham Sect, including its famous leader William Wilberforce, emerged from this Evangelical Revival. The members of this group were primarily influential Anglicans who showed the power of a ministry in which proclamation and demonstration were inseparable. They were instrumental in founding missionary and tract societies, including the British and Foreign Bible Society and the Church Missionary Society. They also worked tirelessly to combat injustices and establish righteousness throughout the world. Their efforts centered on the liberation of slaves, the abolition of the slave trade both in Britain and around the world, and the reform of the penal system. As celebrated by the movie *Amazing Grace*, the year 2006 marked the bicentennial of the abolition of the slave trade in England, the best known of their efforts.

One member of the Clapham Sect, Hannah More, played a significant role among the disadvantaged communities where she served. In *Fierce Convictions*, Karen Swallow Prior profiles how More served her community by establishing banking cooperatives among women who were excluded from the banks. These banking clubs allowed women to save small amounts of money each quarter safely with a larger group. Then, if one of the members of the club lost her job or contracted an illness, she received a payment from the group to help her cope.[4]

During this time, there were many other groups and individuals who combined Word and deed as they battled social evils around the world, such as the opium trade, forced labor, kidnapping, prostitution, the caste system, and infanticide. Missionaries were as well known for their help in medicine, clean water, and agriculture as for their sharing of the Gospel. Bishop John Cheverus, a Catholic priest and community activist, answered the call to move from France to Boston in the 1800s, where he lived among the Native Americans and learned their language, nursed the sick and dying during two yellow fever epidemics, and created a safe place for the working class to save their money. John Livingston Nevius, a Presbyterian missionary in China, introduced the modern orchard industry into Shantung. The Basel missionaries revolutionized the economy of Ghana by introducing coffee and cocoa grown by families and individuals on their own land. James Mc-Kean transformed the life of northern Thailand by helping eliminate its three major curses—smallpox, malaria, and leprosy. Wells and clean water, which helped eliminate many illnesses, often came through the help of missionaries. Throughout the 19th century, missionaries stressed the importance of industrial schools; from there industries were established.[5]

If the biblical and historical Christian response to poverty is a unified emphasis on the Good News and good deeds, why doesn't there seem to be the same level of integration in the efforts of the Church in the U.S. today?

GREAT REVERSALS

As the Evangelical Revival swept through the United States and England, many church leaders tended to have a strong emphasis on just preaching and conversion. A reversal occurred, according to historian Timothy L. Smith in *Revivalism and Social Reform*, when many Christians wanted to concentrate primarily on social needs they believed were being neglected.

For instance, Walter Rauschenbusch, a leader of the Social Gospel movement in the early 1900s, practiced a faith that addressed poverty and injustice, maintaining that a Kingdom of God that is abstracted into some heavenly afterlife is worthless in the slums. "The Kingdom of God is the Christian transfiguration of the social order," Rauschenbusch wrote in 1917 in *A Theology of the Social Gospel*.[6] Such Christians devoted their lives to transforming the earth into a Kingdom of God with no poverty or social injustice.

During this time, Christians and their leaders were also being exposed to the intellectual challenges of Darwinism and secular humanism. For many of these people, the desire to share the "old time religion" receded further and further, while emphasis on dealing with people in the here and now became dominant.

Such an emphasis on the physical reality of the Kingdom meant, in some cases, a near exclusion of the spiritual realm. A purely social message missed key points about the eternal nature of the Kingdom of God and the Gospel. This inevitably sparked a backlash and another reversal from Christians concerned with recovering the spiritual and eternal elements of Christ's message. These believers stressed faith over works and evangelism over relief, and so the pendulum swung back. Many in the Church dismissed the social demands of the Gospel entirely, going instead to the opposite extreme of focusing entirely on the spiritual. As the two camps polarized, an integrated approach to the ministry of Word and deed became harder to grasp.

The growing evangelical movements in the early 1900s illustrated this change as their emphasis on teaching and preaching seemed to portray

PHILIPPINES

these as the only ministries worthy of the Church's time and attention. As one example of that legacy, consider the curriculum of the vast majority of evangelical seminaries—the focus is overwhelmingly on teaching and preaching, and there are few courses devoted to finding innovative and meaningful ways to minister to people physically.

As this shift in emphasis occurred, the primary concern for many Christians became "going to heaven." Over time, Americans—both Christian and otherwise—often acquired the understanding that the singular role of Christianity is to arrive at heaven's gate and to be allowed entry. Although that is certainly something to anticipate with joy, it ignores Jesus' clear, integrated teaching that God's Kingdom exists on earth as well. Jesus taught His followers to pray, "Your kingdom come, your will be done, on earth as it is in heaven" (Matthew 6:10). We are instructed to be simultaneously citizens of a future Kingdom and ambassadors in this time and place. While we wait for a future with Christ, we are called to do everything we can to bring elements of that glorious future into this world. Jesus talked often about a Kingdom that is breaking into this world right now, a Kingdom that isn't marked by opulent buildings but by opulent acts of compassion and kindness. This Kingdom isn't characterized by its military might but by its willingness to kneel down in selfless service.

Bryant L. Myers, a leading voice for Christian engagement with poverty, summarizes this divisive situation:

> So evangelism (restoring people's relationship with God) is spiritual work, while social action (restoring just economic, social, and political relationships among people) is not. In the final analysis this false dichotomy leads Christians to believe that God's redemptive work takes place only in the spiritual realm, while the world is left, seemingly, to the devil. ... Because we have tended to accept the dichotomy between the spiritual and the physical, we sometimes inadvertently limit the scope of both sin and the gospel.[7]

ISN'T THIS THE GOVERNMENT'S RESPONSIBILITY?

The Church's response to poverty in the United States has also been affected by the increased involvement of our federal and state governments in social programs. The social programs instituted to overcome the devastation of the Great Depression, which included Social Security, the G.I. Bill, and other programs following World War II; the Great Society social bills of the 1960s; and many other massive pieces of legislation have created a social safety net. Without commenting on the efficiency or effectiveness of these programs, we can observe that they further distanced the Church in the United States from the job of engaging poverty and other social injustices. The work of addressing physical needs was increasingly seen as government work, while the Church increased its focus on the spiritual realm.

AN UNHELPFUL DICHOTOMY

Modern thought encourages us to think in hierarchical categories. The word *priority* is an illustration of this. Christian organizations, when considering how to budget their time and money, often develop a list of priorities based on the Bible. However, more often than not, the Bible speaks of integrated responsibilities (e.g., faith and works) and tensions (e.g., the Kingdom is both already and not yet here) over priorities. When Jesus was asked to prioritize the commandments, He summarized all the Law and the Prophets in just two: Love God, love your neighbor. Any priority list that doesn't align with these commands will cause us to miss the full picture of what God desires for us.

Consider how the end of the Great Commission passage in Matthew 28:19-20 is often interpreted. Jesus said, "Therefore go and make disciples of all nations, baptizing them in the name of the Father and of the Son and of the Holy Spirit, and teaching them to obey everything I have commanded you." In many instances, this teaching is understood to refer exclusively to *propositional evangelism*. Yet Jesus had something far greater in mind: to follow everything He taught with His words and *with His life*. This passage should point believers toward the ministry model of Jesus, who seamlessly integrated proclamation and practice in His ministry to all people, with special attention paid to the vulnerable and downtrodden.

A WAY FORWARD

Based on Scripture and history, I believe church-based programs are most effective when they simultaneously meet both spiritual and physical needs in a culturally appropriate manner. As we will discuss later, to accomplish this, it might be the case that multiple people and organizations need to work side by side without competition or jealousy. If an integrated approach to making disciples is a scriptural imperative, followers of Christ are not at liberty to choose between proclaiming Christ or serving the needs of the world. While this fact may cause discomfort for Christians for a variety of reasons, we should ultimately rejoice in the many advantages of integrated ministry. Here are a few:

- *Integration increases effectiveness.* The effectiveness of physical ministry and the effectiveness of verbal ministry are each enhanced when done together.[8]

- *Integration reenergizes the Church.* U.S. Christians can rightly be accused of being too inwardly focused. Service is what the Church was designed for, and when we do it, we benefit in many ways.

- *Integration helps correct an image problem.* Christians are often known only for what we are against. Helping people materially provides a way for followers of Jesus to be known for something positive. Leroy Barber, co-founder and executive director of The Voices Project, lays down the gauntlet: "Christian rhetoric without tangible acts of love is hypocrisy."[9]

- ***Integration improves trust and builds relationships.*** Research shows that the majority of Christians came to faith as the result of a relationship.[10] Although not supported by rigorous data analysis, my own experience certainly supports the finding that relationships are the most important factor in people coming to faith.

God's body on earth—the Church—is uniquely able to provide a special feast for people around the world by simultaneously meeting spiritual and physical needs. Many of the Church's characteristics that allow it to function so well in this regard are obvious, such as its physical presence in so many communities around the world. But God provided some additional strategies for the Church to use. Charity is one of those strategies that is not only biblically recommended but also relatively easy to use. Unfortunately, it can also be easily misused.

3

Searching for Solutions That Work

(PETER)

When the Soviet Union disintegrated in 1991, the physical and spiritual needs in this part of the world became evident. Members of a church in Lancaster County, Pennsylvania, asked, "How can we help?" Through the Slavic Gospel Association, they partnered with a church in Zaporozhye, Ukraine, a city of a million people straddling a river in the country's southeast. This was not a distant, impersonal partnership that amounted to sending an annual check. The church leadership and congregation of Lancaster's Calvary Monument Bible Church (CMBC) considered this a true relationship and wanted to find ways of supporting their brothers and sisters overseas. Just as importantly, CMBC wanted to be supported by them in a mutually encouraging relationship.

After an initial assessment trip, the leaders at Calvary Monument identified immediate needs and responded. Recognizing that local food production and distribution were inadequate, they shipped food from Lancaster, a region of fertile farmland. They saw that the Ukrainians wore old clothes often insufficient for the harsh winters. Following Jesus' command that if you have two tunics you should give one away, they shared their clothes with their Ukrainian friends. Hospitals and infirmaries in Zaporozhye had little or no supplies, so CMBC arranged for shipments of medicine and medical supplies donated by area doctors and hospitals. They saw that the Ukrainian believers had only a crowded building in which to worship, so they helped purchase land and provide funds to build additional educational space. This pattern continued for several years, marked annually by a special Thanksgiving offering and shipping container filled with food, clothing, and church supplies. CMBC did everything it could think of to help the church in Zaporozhye, and it was not alone; dozens of other U.S. churches developed relationships with churches throughout the former Soviet Union at this pivotal time in history.

CMBC's response was admirable; it was based on relationship, responsive to seen needs, and generous. But, paradoxically, it was also flawed.

What was wrong? Shouldn't we celebrate such acts of generosity? Shouldn't we encourage many *more* churches to give sacrificially? Before answering these hard questions, we need to continue the story and watch how the relationship between the Lancaster church and the Ukrainian church developed.

PERU

After three years of this partnership, leaders from both sides of the Atlantic Ocean came to the realization that the help from the U.S. church was, at best, insufficient. The Ukrainian church would *always* have needs that the U.S. church could respond to—no amount of giving would change the socioeconomic reality of life in the former Soviet Union.

At worst, the seemingly admirable U.S. support could be harming the Ukrainians. The pastor of the church in Ukraine initially thought it was a blessing to receive generous gifts and support from a church that had no previous ties to his country or people. But he grew increasingly concerned about how this relationship was changing his congregation. He wanted to find a way for his church to become self-sustaining rather that reliant upon distant generosity. He feared his church was becoming increasingly dependent on outside resources and was losing the motivation to serve each other. Why sacrifice anything to feed or clothe a neighbor when an international shipment would soon arrive?

The Ukrainian pastor had other important questions too: What would happen if the generous people in Pennsylvania suddenly stopped providing? Would this kind of assistance produce a stronger community long after the donations stopped? How could the church continue distributing the supplies to those who most needed them?

There were economic repercussions as well. After more investigation, this pastor determined that the well-intentioned generosity of the Lancaster church would likely hurt the incomes of local businesses, which competed with the free goods and services entering their marketplace.

It seemed the gifts from the United States, however well-intentioned, might cause more problems than they solved. Both churches were learning a difficult lesson: Compassionate responses to certain needs work well in the short term but are insufficient for the long term. Effective obedience to the clear biblical command to clothe the naked and give food to the hungry requires asking the question of *how*. It is possible for well-meaning responses to inadvertently strengthen the chains of poverty.

These are hard words for the Church in the United States to hear. The experience of CMBC is not unique. More and more U.S. churches are seeking meaningful ways to serve their brothers and sisters around the world. The convenience and affordability of travel have exposed churchgoers from the United States to formerly unknown people and places. We feel compelled to help. The shock of seeing severe poverty has a way of confronting us with how much we have and how protected we are. This emotional reaction—we have to do *something!*—is a wonderful place to start but an insufficient, and possibly even harmful, place to end.

What makes the story of the Lancaster church somewhat unusual is that some of its members were prepared to respond with their hearts *and* their heads.[1] They didn't let their urge to be compassionate stifle their need to ask and listen to tough questions. They were ready to offer an integrated, correctable response to the issue of poverty. The church leaders recognized that unintended and even unimagined consequences often follow actions.

Consequences are seldom discussed at church functions. After a presentation from a team that just handed out food and clothing on a short-term mission trip, who wants to be the pessimist that points out the potential problems of this act of kindness? Imagine responding to a child's excitement about missions with a statement like, "But what unintended impact will our actions have on the local people and marketplace?" Many would be offended by your challenge to their good intentions. When a church body sincerely pours itself into a service project, nobody wants to doubt the results or imagine there could be negative consequences. Yet the detrimental effects of some of the most minor and well-meaning actions are more common than people want to believe.[2]

There are common pitfalls that trap our churches and organizations when they fight global poverty. It is important to take a serious look at successes and failures and honestly evaluate if our efforts leave communities better off than before our "service."

DEPENDENCY AND DISINCENTIVES

On a trip to Afghanistan with a group of donors, pastors, and development practitioners, I had the once-in-a-lifetime experience of touring northern Afghanistan in a Russian-made helicopter.

I particularly remember one tiny mountain village where we were paraded around by local elders who showed us all their "needs." They brought us to a community center that had some minor water damage to the roof. Outside this building, an elder waved his finger at me, saying, "You must fix this!" Now I'm not particularly handy, yet even I could probably have repaired this small problem with locally available materials and a few hours of sweat. The attitude in that village was that foreigners should be responsible for meeting every need.

Outside assistance had weakened and begun to paralyze local initiative and ownership. As we lifted off, my mind was racing as swiftly as the rotor blades above my head. Surely there must be a better way to participate in addressing the incredible needs in our world.

The attitudes of dependency and disincentive are human—they plague our daily decisions and large-scale development efforts with equal ease. Last year, I heard through the grapevine—okay, my wife spilled the beans—that my in-laws were going to buy me a new watch for Christmas. My watch was on the fritz, and I had to keep tapping it to encourage the second hand to move. Knowing a new watch was coming, there was no way I would spend my own money on a new one, and, crucially, there was no *incentive* to bother fixing it either. In fact, solving the problem myself would have been an act of foolishness in this circumstance.

We perpetuate a terrible lie when we say that individuals living in poverty are "too poor to do anything." Each of us has something to give and some responsibility to use our resources and skills to serve.

Misguided giving can actually rob people living in poverty—not of their physical resources, but of their dignity, responsibility, and self-worth. We cannot afford to waste limited resources that could equip and enable people to rebuild their lives, churches, and communities.

Joel (Wickre) Vikre, founding board member of Blood:Water Mission, warns about how bad the problem can become:

> People who are treated as helpless come to hold a lesser view of themselves. People who believe they are "blessed to be a blessing" and not in need themselves come to a lesser view of the people they serve. These victim and savior complexes create a co-dependency that perpetuates the problems of poverty and far outweighs any temporary relief such missions provide. ... Poor people understand that getting help requires appearing helpless, and rich people unwittingly advance the helplessness of those they serve by seeing them as objects of charity, not equals.[3]

MALAWI

IMPROPER DIAGNOSIS

Several years ago, my grandmother fell ill and was hospitalized. For two weeks, doctors watched over her and ran a battery of tests until they finally discovered she had a medical condition related to her nervous system. Only at this point was it possible to start proper treatment.

The same principle of diagnosis is true for believers involved in overseas projects. How much time is spent diagnosing the causes before imposing solutions? How much time is spent listening to the people we are seeking to serve and developing strong enough relationships so that we can hear their voices? This model of diagnosis does not fit with the U.S. way of taking charge and getting things done. For instance, we often plan the solutions before we embark on a short-term mission trip. We collect our luggage at a foreign airport and jump into projects without sufficiently involving and listening to the local people we are seeking to serve. Mission committees are typically sincere and compassionate, yet the results of their intentions are not always sound because they are based on insufficient information. If we don't understand the problem, how can we implement an appropriate solution? What looks like a good plan in the church boardroom may not seem as wise on the steep streets of a Peruvian village.

A key initial step in understanding a problem is gaining perspective about the local environment and social conditions. A good doctor will first ask probing questions about a patient's family history, health, dietary habits, and personal relationships before making a diagnosis. Similarly, we must approach missions opportunities with a spirit of inquiry. We risk proposing ill-fitting and ill-received solutions if we do not first humble ourselves to learn about the local culture and respect the local people.

A Christian author, well known for his bestselling book on praying for prosperity, made just such a mistake. After selling millions of copies of his book on prospering through prayer, Bruce Wilkinson moved his family to South Africa and launched a nonprofit organization to help Africans suffering from HIV/AIDS. The centerpiece of his efforts was to have been a grand theme park in Swaziland—including a golf course, cannery, chicken farm, schools, and churches, among other things—that would cater to Western tourists and house 10,000 AIDS orphans. Despite cautions from the U.S. ambassador, who warned Wilkinson that uprooting orphans from their communities went against Swazi culture, Wilkinson forged ahead. He gave the Swazi king five days to approve a plan that would give his nonprofit organization a 99-year lease on prime game parks, forcing out local environmental groups that had controlled the parks for decades.[4]

When the Swazi press caught wind of Wilkinson's proposal, they detected a scent of colonialism. Justified or not, the Swazi media turned popular opinion against the project. When he failed to get the king's approval for the tracts of land, Wilkinson quit the project and returned to the U.S., explaining that Swazi traditions had failed to adequately provide for the multitudes of AIDS orphans, and that drastic new measures and bold dreams were required. Wilkinson's heart may have been in the right place, but how would things have turned out if he had adequately engaged the local population and listened to their ideas before proposing his solutions?

CONFUSING RELIEF WITH DEVELOPMENT

A helpful first step in thinking about working with families in need in any context is to discern whether the situation calls for relief, development, or some combination of the two.[5] Relief is a rapid provision of temporary resources to reduce immediate suffering. When we see need, we think of providing relief. James 2:16 questions, "If one of you says to [those with physical needs], 'Go in peace; keep warm and well fed,' but does nothing about their physical needs, what good is it?"

I found myself in this situation several years ago in Haiti. We were visiting a small village and saw a small child with sores on his body and fluid coming out of his ears. When we asked the mother if she had visited the hospital, she responded, "Yes, but I just didn't have the funds required for the prescription." Looking at her other children, her house, and her surroundings, we knew she was telling the truth. What must it be like to know how to heal your child but to have no way of coming up with a modest amount of money for critical medicine? We knew the urgency of this situation required an immediate response. The knowledge that we were engaged in bringing longer-term sustainable economic development to her community did nothing for the immediate need of her sick child. We secretly gave the necessary money to a local staff member and asked him to ensure that this child received proper treatment.

Despite occasions like this when short-term immediate aid is required, we know that longer-term development is a preferable response. Certainly it would be better if this mother had an income sufficient to guarantee that if her kids fall sick she will be able to pay for their treatment. Giles Bolton, a veteran African diplomat, describes the difference between relief and development: "In consumer language, [development] is a bit like making an investment rather than an immediate purchase. ... [It's a] much better value if it works because it gives poor people control over their own lives and enables them better to withstand future humanitarian disasters without outside help."[6]

Both relief and development can be appropriate interventions, but if we *sustain* relief efforts instead of transitioning to longer-term development, we hurt the very people we are trying to help.

UNINTENDED CONSEQUENCES

After the 1994 genocide in Rwanda, many Christian organizations were motivated to rebuild this broken country. Following the example and admonitions of Jesus to feed the hungry, clothe the naked, and show compassion to the hurting, these organizations and their dedicated people responded. Churches in the United States rebuilt Rwandan churches and schools, sent food aid and supplies, and attempted to address the unimaginable physical and psychological damage inflicted by the hundred days of terror. Several years after the genocide, peace and stability allowed Rwanda to transition from a country needing emergency assistance to one needing long-term development. Unfortunately, many churches and aid organizations failed to recognize this, leading to frustrations like those experienced by a Rwandan named Jean.

After the genocide, Jean seized an opportunity to begin a small poultry business to provide his neighborhood with eggs. He managed to scrape together funds to purchase several fowl, and his business grew. Later, a church in the United States "adopted" the village where Jean lived and worked. The church decided to donate clothes and supplies. They also imported eggs from a neighboring community and gave them away. Suddenly, this one village was flooded with sur-plus eggs. It is not difficult to imagine what happened to Jean's business: People went first to collect the free eggs and bought Jean's eggs only when the supply of free eggs was depleted. The market price for eggs plummeted in Jean's village, and, as a result, Jean was forced to sell his productive assets, his chickens.

The next year, after Jean had left the poultry business, the church that had supplied the free eggs turned its attention to another disaster in another part of the world. Jean's community had no capacity to produce eggs locally and was forced to import eggs from a neighboring town. The cost of these eggs was higher than the eggs Jean had sold, so both Jean and his village were hurt economically by the good intentions of one U.S. church.

Have you ever donated your used T-shirts to your local thrift store? Often these are bundled and shipped to Africa. This business of secondhand Western clothing, called the *mivumba* trade in East Africa, decimated clothing production in countries like Uganda and Zambia that previously had thriving textile industries. Several other countries, including Nigeria and Eritrea, have imposed significant tariffs on foreign imports to avoid a similar fate.[7] It is hard to comprehend that our used T-shirts could harm local producers on another continent, yet the Church in the United States must learn to be aware of such consequences in our increasingly interconnected world.

FOCUS ON THE FOREIGNERS

If we were to hold an impartial mirror to our hearts, we would have to admit that sometimes our "noble" actions are self-serving. We in the West who have been so blessed with material wealth often feel guilty about our relative prosperity and good fortune compared with our distant brothers and sisters in developing countries. Guilt can motivate us to "bless others as we have been blessed." And yet we face a serious problem if we act out of a desire for clear consciences that enable us to continue living in abundance.

I hosted a group of church members who traveled to Rwanda to visit programs related to HIV/AIDS prevention, maternal health, and economic development that they had been supporting for several years. As we drove around the hilly countryside, they tossed handfuls of candy out the window at random groups of Rwandans they passed. They were filled with happiness at the thought that they were bringing joy to this country and making a difference. The local staff members were embarrassed, but they kept silent because they did not want to offend their guests. These local staff members knew actions like this transform some hardworking Rwandans into beggars and exacerbate the poor dental health of the region.

CONNECTING HEADS AND HEARTS

After hearing about the unintended consequences of very good intentions and reflecting on our own culpability, it might be easy to slip toward hopelessness and discouragement. "We're just trying to help!" a friend complained after seeing a missions project fail. "I didn't know it was going to be so hard. ... I feel like giving up." Something in us knows it isn't right to turn a blind eye to the enormous needs in our world—that doesn't square with the biblical teaching on compassion and action. But just as inaction is not an option for followers of Christ, neither should we act inappropriately. We want to do more than just care about people living in poverty—we want to help families flourish.

We are required to do the hard work of continually evaluating our actions and determining what is most helpful to the people we're seeking to serve.

It is necessary to connect heads and hearts and to fully engage both for God's glory. There is a problem if we have one without the other. Our desire is to see the Church move from well-intentioned blunders to thoughtful, compassionate acts of mercy that result in true flourishing.

WHERE NOW?

If there were easy ways to alleviate poverty, we would have found them by now. Collectively, the world has spent $3.2 trillion of government aid on international development programs since 1960.[8] Finally we're beginning to wonder: Where are the results? It's time for the Church to ask the same question. After all of the good intentions, where are the results? Have our good intentions truly made an impact on poverty and expanded Christ's Kingdom around the world?

If funding were all that was required, many more of the world's problems would be solved by now. Increased funding will neither end global poverty nor fulfill the Church's mandate. There is a growing consensus that different approaches and tools are needed for the Church to effectively care for the spiritual and physical needs of those living in poverty.

Thankfully, we have successful models of a different approach. I think of a rural church in Rwanda where I met Anasitaziya. Unable to see, nearly 80 years old, and widowed during the genocide, she may have seemed like a likely candidate for charity. But Anasitaziya did not let her circumstances limit her. She grows beans and potatoes for a living, hiring people to help her do the work. In 2011, she began saving just 71 cents a month through her local church. After she and her group built up a lump sum of money, she took out a loan to buy materials to repair her home, which had been in danger of collapsing. "I may be old. I may be blind," she told me, "but I have built my house and now rent out rooms. I will not beg. I will provide for my family."

What separates examples like Anasitaziya from the pitfalls previously described? One of the main differences is that employment builds hope, produces dignity, and creates a sustainable solution to poverty.

RWANDA

4

A Hand Up, Not a Handout

(PETER)

Marcel, a friend from Rwanda, wrote an email stating, "I am not good because there has been a long time without a job. I am still looking for a job. My life is not going well for me." Marcel was not making a veiled plea for a handout; he truly wanted an opportunity to use his skills and abilities to provide for his needs. The more time we spend listening to the people we are trying to serve, the more we will hear Marcel's refrain repeated in various contexts and within various cultures—people living in poverty know that a handout is inferior to an opportunity to work and provide for one's own long-term needs. Nearly every human prefers the dignity that comes from employment to the demeaning dependence of handouts.

In the United States, we often have a skewed view of work. We might complain about our coworkers, the coffee, the cost of health care, and the lack of vacation. We might complain about our boss and the buzzing of the lights. With all this complaining, we might start to believe that our job is a curse.

Work is *not* a curse. God worked as He created the universe. Adam and Eve had plenty of work to do in caring for the Garden. All of this work occurred before sin entered the world. Properly understood, work is a blessing. If you don't believe me, ask someone in the developing world who doesn't have a job. That individual will be able to describe the harm that results from

unemployment and how the absence of employment is a much more significant curse than whatever "cursed" job you might have.

A look at the example of ancient Israel and the history of the United States
supports the assertion that employment is the best way to address long-term
physical poverty.

BIBLICAL MODEL

Ancient Israel had a systematic code governing the care of those in poverty.
Israel understood what it was like to be oppressed as a result of their bondage in Egypt. Shortly after their miraculous exodus, God provided a system
of laws that codified their care for those in need.

In the book of Ruth, we see a successful businessman, Boaz, cultivating his
fields but taking special care to leave some of the field for Ruth, a widow and
foreigner from Moab. Boaz was following the requirement in Deuteronomy
24:19: "When you are harvesting in your field and you overlook a sheaf, do
not go back to get it. Leave it for the foreigner, the fatherless and the widow,
so that the Lord your God may bless you in all the work of your hands." This
law was echoed in the ancient rabbinic tradition: "One who prevents the poor
from gathering gleanings or allows one poor person to gather and prevents
another from doing so, is deemed a robber of the poor."[1]

In addition to this specific command, other Old Testament laws governed
the ability to reclaim lost land so that individuals could return to work, mandated that wages be paid promptly, and ensured that a high level of care was
provided to employees. Notice that these specific laws were designed to
protect employment opportunities, not facilitate endless handouts. For example, in "sharing the harvest," a widow or foreigner was required to do the
gathering and the threshing. Work was still required.

In the New Testament, Paul warns the church in Thessalonica: "The one
who is unwilling to work shall not eat" (2 Thessalonians 3:10) and sets the
expectation that everyone capable of working should provide for themselves

INDIA

and their families. He recognized that giving aid to individuals who have the capacity to work could deprive those who truly need resources. Paul himself lived this principle as he sewed tents and labored so that he would not be a burden to supporting churches. To the Ephesians, Paul writes, "Anyone who has been stealing must steal no longer, but must work, doing something useful with their own hands, that they may have something to share with those in need" (Ephesians 4:28). In this situation, employment is the tool that helps turn robbers into generous givers.

These are just a few examples of a broader theme woven throughout Scripture that the preferred system to care for people in poverty is one that uses God-given abilities in productive employment.

HISTORICAL EXAMPLES

The historical record of giving in the United States shows a model similarly focused on employment and responsibility instead of handouts.

When the U.S. was founded, it was considered immoral to give aid to those who had the capacity to work. This would be robbing those who truly needed resources, thus harming the people the aid was meant to help. Cotton Mather, the influential Puritan minister, stated in 1698, "I will rather utter an exhortation ... that you may not abuse your charity by misapplying it."[2] Mather recognized that charity has the potential to do enormous good for people who need it, but that the greatest threat to charity could be those who indiscriminately give without appropriately engaging and involving the recipient.

DEMOCRATIC REPUBLIC OF CONGO

At that point in our nation's history, when an individual asked for assistance, the first response was to look at the situation. If the individual had the ability to work, then he or she was given work. And there was certainly plenty to do in the "New World." Food-for-work programs began, and hostels for people in need almost always required some sort of contribution. The idea of someone "mooching" was intolerable, and aid was cautiously distributed only after the individual's situation was evaluated. Cotton Mather succinctly encouraged his congregation to find employment for those in poverty. "Find 'em work; set 'em to work; keep 'em to work."[3]

As the United States prospered, giving grew exponentially. The early 1900s saw a particularly high growth rate of charitable giving; between 1911 and 1925, 16 of the largest cities increased their relief payments from $1.6 million to $14.7 million, a 918 percent increase.[4] With this growth came a professionalization and delocalization of giving, as well as a slow shift away from employment-producing programs. When the Great Depression hit, President Franklin D. Roosevelt hoped that his New Deal responses would be only a temporary solution. In November 1933 he stated, "When any man or woman goes on a dole something happens to them mentally and the quicker they are taken off the dole the better it is for them the rest of their lives."[5] Many of the New Deal programs were designed not around entitlement but on employment. Charity was, and is, best seen as a temporary assistance to bridge the gap between need and employment.

Unfortunately, many U.S. churches have slipped into a charity mindset and do not follow the historical or the scriptural example. This shift away from employment has unintentionally crippled the Church's long-term impact on poverty.

THE BENEFITS OF EMPLOYMENT OVER CHARITY

Do you remember how you felt when you received your first paycheck? In middle school I mowed elderly Mrs. Johnson's lawn. She would inspect my work and acknowledge that I had cut close enough to her barn and not missed any sections under her apple trees. Then she would invite me into her house, offer me a cold Tang mixed with her special spices, and pay me for my work. I enjoyed a strong sense of satisfaction as she thanked me for a job well done.

Relying on charity might provide enough for a bare existence, but it will never be enough to help someone off their knees. Charity will never allow an individual to flourish in the way God created humankind to be—productive in caring for the earth and using the strength and skills He gave. And besides, charity isn't what those living in poverty want.

We've all heard the saying, "If you give a man a fish, you feed him for a day, but if you teach a man to fish, you feed him for life." These well-worn words contain an important truth: Who would settle for an occasional fish dropped off on their doorstep if they had the opportunity to start their own fishing business?

Drawing on his personal experience with the Waodoni tribe, missionary Steve Saint writes, "We may be the wealthiest nation and the wealthiest Christians on earth, but that is not a good reason to give someone something." Saint goes on to describe the following challenges that come from long-term handouts:

- *No value:* It is much more difficult to appreciate the value of something that costs us nothing. Consequently, it does not last as long.

- *Personal devaluation:* If people are always given things, they begin to expect them, thereby negating personal dreams or aspirations of climbing out of their current condition. Always being on the receiving end encourages people to see themselves as incompetent, unable to learn even if they did decide they wanted to learn.

- *Desire becomes necessity:* Giving a gift to one person can result in everyone else wanting one as well. Similar but more critical is the possibility that if the first gift proves effective, there will suddenly be a legitimate need for many more. And if you cannot give the same tool to everyone, it is better not to give it to anyone. Help make it affordable, and then everyone can buy their own.[6]

FLYING KITES

When we engage in employment-based solutions, the benefits of employment extend to future generations. Outside a small office in Trou-du-Nord, Haiti, I saw several boys with homemade kites. Using a plastic bag, some string, and a few sticks, these three boys constructed kites capable of expertly navigating tangled power lines and two-story buildings. I could see other kids watching and learning from their example. Other children saw what was possible, and there grew a prestige factor in who could get his kite the highest.

In the same way, I've seen community members improve their lives, motivating other community members to action through their hard work. If my neighbors can pull their families out of poverty, why can't I? Essentially, they are pushing the limits of what is possible, and from very little they are making kites that can fly higher and higher.

MOLDOVA

Employment decreases the need for never-ending support. There is an exit strategy for any external assistance provided. Many churches are beginning to recognize that their international assistance has built churches, trained pastors, fed the hungry ... and somehow created a web of dependency from which there is no way out. They have not built the surrounding economic infrastructure to ensure the longevity of these worthy efforts.

Contrast this type of situation with Jacob Timos' experience in Moldova. While Moldova is one of the poorest countries in Europe, with almost 22 percent of Moldovans living below the poverty line, Jacob is an example of someone using business to help both his family and community move forward. In 2004, Jacob took out a $400 loan from Invest-Credit, a local, Christ-centered organization, to buys six rabbits. Since then, Jacob has used subsequent loans to expand his business, and he currently sells over 300 rabbits a year, both in Moldova and in neighboring European countries.

Jacob uses his business to minister to others. Rather than focusing on competition, Jacob donates rabbits to other families interested in starting their own business. He builds a partial refund into his business model and asks customers to donate this amount to their local church. This surprising policy leads many of his customers to ask questions, prompting several conversations about faith. One customer heard the Gospel when she went to church to donate the refunded money—and then accepted Christ! A pastor as well as a farmer, Jacob deeply believes in the power of business to create change: "So many believers run businesses here, create jobs for others, and provide services for the community."

WHERE TO BEGIN?

If gifts don't create long-term change, and handouts tend to keep people on their knees, and if lasting solutions for families in poverty come through employment, does that let us off the hook? Absolutely not! We have the potential to play a critical role in advancing employment opportunities and helping those in poverty dramatically improve their lives.

But how? What can you and I do that actually helps? First we need to understand what it would be like to be born in rural Siem Riep, Cambodia. Over a decade ago, I briefly worked in this town situated a day's boat ride north of the capital, Phnom Penh, and it provided my first glimpse into rural poverty. Every day after work, I would jump on a moped and speed away to watch the sunset from the pinnacles of the temples of Angkor Wat, the "Asian pyramids." On my drive there, I would pass farmers wading in rice fields, planting, and I would try to understand what life would be like if I were born into their situation.

If you were born to a rural farm family and stopped your education at the fourth grade, how could you secure one of the competitive positions of formal employment? How would you even know about job openings? You wouldn't receive a newspaper. You wouldn't post your résumé on LinkedIn. If you weren't related to someone already inside an organization that offered formal employment or didn't have sufficient savings to bribe your way in, you wouldn't have a chance.

In many developing countries, if you did receive a job offer, you would be required to pay a "deposit." The practice of requiring deposits is one of the most oppressive systems for employees in poverty. Outside Pune, India, rural laborers are paid 85 cents per day and yet are required to provide a deposit of up to $50 without any documentation or guarantee that these funds will be returned when their employment ends.

Consider the reality of life for men and women living in poverty. What could you do to earn money beyond your meager wages from subsistence agriculture or day labor for an oppressive employer? Your only option would be to create your own employment. What would you do to provide a better life for your children? How would you start? What would you need?

PART II

How Christ, Community, and Capital Can Change the World

5

Unlocking Entrepreneurship

(PETER)

You don't have to be an economist to understand capital. Consider Abdul Saboor. Abdul runs a small television repair business in Kabul, Afghanistan. He received a small loan to increase his inventory of spare parts and hire two additional people to help manage his growing business, significantly improving his efficiency. "I used to have to go to the market [by foot] every day to buy parts," he said, adding that it was a 2½-hour round trip. "Now I go once every two weeks."[1]

He used a loan to open a second shop, which increased his sales and thus his profits. More importantly, he increased his efficiency and productivity and provided jobs for two more people.

ECONOMIC STIMULUS

Access to capital can unlock the enterprising potential inherent within every individual. Capital empowers men and women in poverty, allowing them to improve their bargaining power and leverage, which can lead to lower costs, higher productivity, and an improved standard of living. According to Peruvian economist Hernando de Soto, "Capital is the force that raises the productivity of labor and creates the wealth of nations. ... It is the foundation of progress and the one thing that poor countries cannot seem to produce themselves, no matter how eagerly their people engage in all the other activities that characterize a capitalist economy."[2]

Stated simply, it takes money to make money. The usual two ways to access that initial capital are through a savings account or a loan. If you ask individuals from virtually any culture who have succeeded in business, you will nearly always hear a story about their first loan that helped put them on the path to building a successful business.

The benefits of capital seem obvious enough to Americans—and we're usually able to acquire the capital we need. Banks, financing companies, and affluent relatives abound in the U.S. and other high-income countries. However, 2 billion people around the world don't have access to financial services, most of them in developing countries.[3] How can entrepreneurs in poverty access modest amounts of capital with which to start and grow their businesses?

REPUBLIC OF CONGO

LOANS

One day, the mail carrier brought me three offers from credit card companies. One touted double airline miles, another guaranteed zero percent interest for all balance transfers for the life of the loan, and another boasted about the size of loan I was prequalified to receive. None of the offers interested me, and I quickly threw them out. However, during my lunch break, I visited Home Depot and was approached by a woman wearing an orange apron covered with badges. Linda offered me $20 or 10 percent off my purchase if I signed on a dotted line and accepted a Home Depot credit card. Now *that* was an offer I couldn't refuse—$20 was enough money to help pay a babysitter so I could have an evening out with my wife!

My ubiquitous access to easy and relatively affordable credit could not be further away from the reality of individuals living in Parola, Philippines. When we visited this high-crime area, the going rate for moneylenders was 20 percent. Not a bad interest rate—until we realized that this rate was for four days! Apparently theft in this area did not just result from robbers and pickpockets; it also came through usurious interest rates on capital and individuals who preyed on those with no other options.

In many parts of the world, "5-6" loans are the norm. Individuals borrow five units and repay six, equaling a 20 percent interest rate. Again, the problem is that this rate is either daily, weekly, or monthly, depending on the particular loan shark. How would it be possible to escape a vicious loan cycle with rates this high? Consider a loan of $100, perhaps used to take a sick relative to the city for medical treatment. At 20 percent weekly interest, that $100 loan could quickly grow to a staggering $1,849 after just 16 weeks. It would be an inescapable trap for all who fall into it.

Later we'll describe innovative ways individuals and organizations access much more reasonably priced capital. But if rates for loans are so ridiculously high for many, perhaps savings is a better route to accumulate the modest amount of capital necessary to launch a business.

SAVINGS

There are many benefits to saving instead of taking a loan. Saving is less risky and more flexible, allowing people to accumulate money to invest in a business or provide for emergencies. So why doesn't everyone save? Our situation in the West differs markedly from the experience of the majority of the world. I remember opening my first savings account with my father at Middlesex Bank on Main Street in Concord, Massachusetts, and how I began saving small amounts. I put an advertisement in the local paper expressing my willingness to work hard and do any odd jobs. Within a week, I was flooded with opportunities to move pianos, paint sheds, haul rocks, and mow lawns. Each week, I would first tithe then put a portion in savings at Middlesex Bank. Slowly these savings grew, and I remember my excitement at having accumulated enough in my account to purchase my first mountain bike.

Contrast my experience to Geetha, who in seven months will need 1,000 Indian rupees—about $15—for school fees for her daughter. She makes $17 a month, so if she doesn't start saving the money now, she'll never have such a large sum.[4]

No banks or formal services are available to Geetha. So, to save for her daughter's school fees, she agrees to save with Jyothi, her friendly neighborhood "savings collector." Jyothi has recognized the need for a safe place to save money and has developed a business to meet that demand. Jyothi goes to Geetha and her other clients each day to collect savings deposits from them. In this way, Geetha saves 5 rupees a day. After doing this for 220 days, Geetha will have deposited 1,100 rupees, and she will then get back 1,000. Jyothi keeps 100 as her fee for providing this valuable service.

Geetha has saved the 1,000 rupees needed to pay her daughter's school fees—but by getting back less than she put in, she actually *paid* to save! How much has Geetha paid to save for the school fees for her daughter? She's paid 30 percent annual percentage rate.[5] Can you imagine? We Americans *earn* money on our savings, while Geetha and others in similar situations are forced to pay for the privilege. And many in the world do not even have access to a savings collector.

Conducting a study to determine if HOPE International should expand its services to a rural fishing village on the Congo River, our group asked several residents a simple question: "If you only have a little money to save, what choices do you have?" Most said they have only one option—travel to the center of the next town and deposit their funds at a savings kiosk. And when they withdraw savings from the kiosk, they pay 10 percent of the maximum balance. One of the potential savers I met would be required to pay 15 cents for transportation plus a 10 percent fee to save $1. If he wanted to save $1 a week for six months, he just paid $6.50, or 25 percent of his total savings, for the privilege. What an incredible negative savings rate!

My first reaction to hearing these high rates was, "That's crazy! Why pay someone to collect and hold your savings for you? Why don't those in poverty just do it themselves, especially when this type of savings arrangement isn't even FDIC insured?" This is a common response to learning that people in poverty like Geetha often pay deposit collectors 30 percent APR in order to save in a place that is only marginally secure and not protected from inflation.

The key to making sense of this is to recognize the enormous obstacles to saving in developing countries. These obstacles are related to the following:

- The reality of living conditions (no place to safely hide cash)
- The enormous social demands of communal societies
- The lack of nearby alternatives

Reality of Living Conditions

If you lived in a five-by-eight-foot tin house with no doors or windows and practically no furniture, where would you hide your cash? How would you protect against theft? Natural disasters can literally burn, rot, or sweep away the cash savings people have tried to squirrel away in hiding places in or near their homes. Pakistan's severe floods of 2010 provide an example, when heavy monsoons damaged or destroyed approximately 1.6 million homes, leaving some 14 million people homeless. As they fled, many people reported seeing money floating by, likely savings that had been hidden in people's homes. "I had nearly 100,000 rupees [about $1,176] in cash buried in an earthen jar under the mud floor of my home," shared Muhammad Rafiq, whose home was destroyed in the flooding. "There was confusion as we fled, and I thought my wife had retrieved it. But we both failed to do so, and now the money has gone."[6]

Societal Demands

In many developing countries, familial and communal ties are so strong it would be social suicide to deny someone money if you have some to spare. Those who have even a little are expected to share with a brother, aunt, cousin, or neighbor who asks. Denying the request would lead to ostracism from the community. Although there are great benefits to a society that shares so completely, it holds people back from accumulating and investing capital—and thus moving forward economically. It is often a question of short-term gain at the cost of long-term progress—or money used for relief instead of development, as we discussed earlier.

Lack of Nearby Alternatives

If I need to deposit money in my bank, I can use my phone or choose from several branches or ATMs within 10 minutes of my home. However, in Rwanda, for example, despite great improvements in account ownership, the average person is still a 53-minute journey from a bank branch or ATM.[7] A trip to the bank would mean two hours of lost business. Interestingly, mobile phones are helping make banking much more accessible in remote areas, with the average Rwandan only 31 minutes away from a mobile money agent. We'll discuss these developments more in Chapter 8.

DOMINICAN REPUBLIC

ALTERNATIVE PIGGY BANKS

So how *do* families in poverty save? Out of necessity, they have created a number of innovative—though not always ideal—options.

On a trip to Santiago, Dominican Republic, I met a woman who manufactures bamboo savings logs. She cuts 12-inch lengths of naturally hollow bamboo stems, seals both ends, and then cuts small slits through which money can be deposited. She described how most customers bury them or hide them underneath a piece of furniture. When asked if they ever put them under their mattresses, she laughed and cautioned, "*Everyone* knows that's where people hide extra money, so you really shouldn't hide your money there."

ZIMBABWE

Another creative savings method was discovered by a British nongovernmental organization operating in Cambodia. At one point, its leaders noticed that many Cambodians raise pigs, so they concluded that it must be a profitable business. Perhaps they could help even more Cambodians take advantage of pig farming. However, after talking with several pig farmers and running the numbers, they were bewildered—the local farmers were *losing* money on their pigs! The cost of raising the pigs exceeded the income received when the pigs were sold. What was going on?

Further research revealed the truth: The Cambodian farmers were raising pigs as a way to save a "lump sum" of money that could be used for school fees, weddings, or to grow their business.

One Cambodian farmer explained it this way: "If I don't have a pig to raise, each day I'll fritter away whatever money I have, partly by responding to the requests of relatives and friends. In three months, I'll have nothing more than I do now. However, if I have a pig, I *have* to take care of it. I have to invest my daily loose change into the pig—I can't allow it to starve or get ill and die. After a few months of this, I'll sell it and use the money for my son's school fees."[8] This farmer was using a literal piggy bank that could protect his money from constantly diminishing.

This farmer's loss on his pig enterprise is similar to the savings fees paid by Geetha, the woman who "earned" a negative 30 percent on her savings. She paid that much to her deposit collector to enjoy the benefits of a future lump sum.

OTHER BENEFITS OF SAVINGS

It might seem counterintuitive, but individuals living in poverty can't afford *not* to save. There are few governmental safety nets in developing countries. Small emergencies can become disasters. Dave Larson, international development expert, describes savings this way:

> Those living in poverty are like someone on the edge of a steep, tall cliff. Perilously near the edge, it won't take much of a blow to force them over the edge into a tragic fall. A fire, a flood, a drought, an illness, an accident—these and other traumas could easily result in catastrophe. Savings helps people reduce their vulnerability. In effect, it allows them to take a few steps away from the edge. Farther away, they are at less risk. A blow may push them toward the edge—but not over. When we help people to save money we're saving lives—in less dramatic but perhaps far more effective ways than we see in the movies. Rather than arriving in a helicopter to grab someone dangling from tree roots atop a cliff, we're helping them to stay away from the tree roots in the first place.

Mike Cahill, a homebuilder from Pennsylvania, traveled to the Dominican Republic to visit Esperanza International. In one small community outside San Pedro, Mike and the team visited Yaquelia, a woman who had just joined Esperanza. When Mike asked Yaquelia about her family, she told the group about her 5-year-old son, Juan, who was suffering from hydrocephalus, a buildup of fluid in the brain. It was obvious that this was a severe medical need and that Juan needed to be treated. Upon returning to the United States, Mike did everything he could to get medical treatment for Juan, even finding a doctor willing to perform the surgery. Unfortunately, after medical examination, they determined that it was too late to treat this abnormality. The tragedy is that Juan could have been cured if his mother had had the knowledge and money to get this treatment in time.

This tragic situation is repeated throughout the world. U2's Bono calls this sort of situation "stupid poverty" and wonders why thousands of individuals should die every day from mosquito bites, starvation, and preventable diseases.[9] There simply is no good reason why 16,000 children should die each day.[10] Poverty is behind almost every one of those unnecessary deaths, and in countless cases, a small savings account could have prevented tragedy.

Ephraim Kabaija, former chief of staff to President Paul Kagame of Rwanda, explained the critical need for a bank that offers savings accounts to the Rwandan people:

> Do you know how many children die in our country every year because their mothers cannot afford the $2 to $10 needed to buy medicines to treat diarrhea, fever, malaria, and other common illnesses? Do you appreciate how much angst, misery, and despair we could eliminate from our country if every family had $50 in a savings account?[11]

PREPARING FOR THE FUTURE

For many in the developing world, everything revolves around *today*. What will I eat today? What will I wear today? Where will I find employment today? Beginning to accumulate savings helps shift an individual's focus from today to tomorrow. A family's timeline begins to change. The emotional benefits of this are hard to quantify, but a street vendor in the Democratic Republic of Congo summarized it best: "I'm not so afraid of tomorrow anymore."

The reality is that having a safe place to save small amounts of capital or access a loan is essential if people are to escape poverty and build a better future. But if the answer isn't national banks or deposit collectors or high-interest loans, what is it?

6

A Brass Ring

(PHIL)

I treasure a photograph of my daughter on an antique carousel near the River Seine in Paris. In the background, the Eiffel Tower is an iron miracle looming in a peacock blue sky. Laura is 12—still young enough to delight unselfconsciously in the lively music and bright colors. She is laughing as she talks my recently retired father into joining her on one of the bright red horses.

A century ago, the operators of these rotating machines would place a brass ring on an iron arm and swing it just out of reach of the outside row of children. If a child could somehow grasp the ring as they went by, they would get a prize. From that practice we get the phrase "grabbing the brass ring." Millions of people in poverty have grabbed their brass rings from a very different type of merry-go-round.

Families living in the developing world desperately need both secure ways to save money and access to affordable credit. These are essential needs, and people have long found innovative ways to save and borrow lump sums of cash, including the method discussed below. Don't be fooled, as I once was, by the simplicity of the method. For two years I dismissed it as unimportant, but I've come to believe it is one of the most powerful ways to help many people in poverty, especially if churches are involved.

I have learned that great power is found in simplicity—the simplicity of a merry-go-round. To illustrate this, consider the following fictional example of how friends and relatives join together to empower one another.

Anna and Bonita invite their best friends, Clara and Delores, to join them in forming a savings group. They agree to meet at Anna's house for the next four Saturday nights, and each will bring $1. Each week they will put a total of $4 in a separate jar, and at the end of four weeks they will each take home a jar with $4 in it. The plan works well. At the end of four weeks, each one has saved $4 from their income.

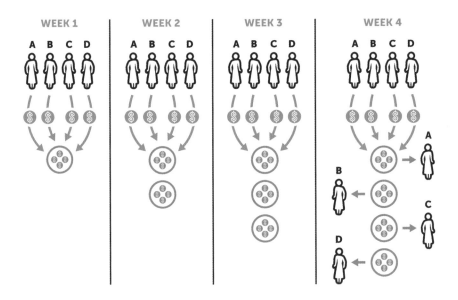

It doesn't take too long for the women to see that it is both insecure and wasteful to keep money hidden in jars, so they agree to rotate who takes the jars home each week. After a drawing to determine turns, Anna takes home the first filled jar, Bonita the second, Clara the third, and Delores the fourth. Again, at the end of four weeks, each one has a jar with $4 in it. The same ending, but something was dramatically different in the two cases because of when they received their jars.

In the second case, Anna's jar essentially contained $1 saved from her income plus $3 of loans from the others. The $3 of loans was repaid over the next three weeks out of her income. Bonita's jar (week two) essentially contained $1 saved from her income, $1 of repayment from Anna, and $2 of loans from Clara and Delores. Clara's jar (week three) contained $1 saved from her income, $2 of repayments from Anna and Bonita, and a $1 loan from Delores. Since Delores was last, her jar contained $3 of repayments from the others plus $1 saved from her income.

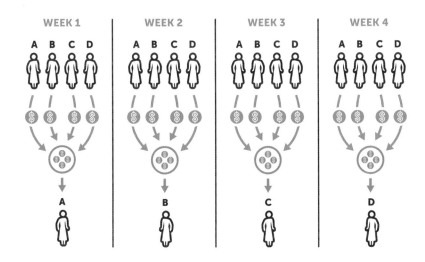

By working together and trusting each other, the women found a way to provide themselves loans and a way to save. In reality, those winning early places in the draw receive special benefits of loans. The ones late in the draw have to take additional risk. Only commitment and social pressure cause the early recipients of the jars to continue putting in their $1 every week. In a later example, I will show you how people have found a way to reduce this risk.

When each woman receives her jar, she then has several options. She can continue to save the money by keeping it in the jar, she can invest the money in her business, or she can choose to spend the money on household needs. She will make those choices depending on her needs and opportunities. One thing she must do, however, is make sure she can finish making the remainder of her $1 payments. The risks of the four women were limited since the obligation lasted for only four weeks. The most risk any of them took was the $3 Delores loaned to the others in the first three weeks.

This type of club has another important benefit hidden from most independently minded Americans. In a typical developing country, each person has a clear responsibility to care for family members, friends, and neighbors. If a person is able to accumulate any money, that person has a corresponding obligation to give or loan that money to someone else in need. This makes it nearly impossible for them to acquire any savings. However, if someone is committed to give money to a group, they have a higher social responsibility to fulfill that commitment, which outweighs all but true emergencies.

These types of groups are most commonly known as ROSCAs (rotating savings and credit associations). Other names include community-managed loan funds, community-managed microfinance, and village savings and loan associations. Locally, they may have other names, such as *consorcios* or *tandas* in Latin America, merry-go-rounds in Africa (having local names like *tontines* or *njangis*), and self-help groups in many parts of India. For the purposes of this book, we will use the term savings and credit association (SCA) to refer to any type of community group in which members save and lend their own money together.

You can already see some advantages of SCAs over other lending and savings methods typically available to people in poverty. Although it may choose to do so, an SCA does not have to charge a fee to save like a savings collector does, nor does it have to charge any interest or fees like moneylenders or banks do. And any interest or fees the group chooses to collect will remain within the group, rather than going to an outside institution.

Variations on SCAs have been around for hundreds of years, sometimes even in mission work. William Carey, the cobbler missionary to India who is recognized as the "father of modern missions," used SCAs in the late 1700s in India to empower women. Carey agreed with Solomon that unless individuals have the power to save, they risk forever being slaves to lenders (Proverbs 22:7).

Yet as useful as these small groups are, their power expands exponentially as more members are added and other tweaks are made, as we'll discuss in the following sections.

BURUNDI

EXPANDING THE MODEL

Let's continue learning from Anna and her friends. Finding their savings group to be helpful, the four women invite 48 neighbors to join them. Again, they agree to draw numbers, and again the draw amazingly comes out in alphabetical order. Anna draws #1, Bonita draws #2, and the others draw until Zoca draws #52. At the end of one year, all of them have saved $52, since they all made 52 $1 payments out of their incomes. However, Anna received the equivalent of a $51 loan, and all the others except Zoca got loans of decreasing amounts. As they received their payments, the members could invest in their businesses, save, or meet personal needs. By trusting each other and meeting their obligations, the members created and shared immense value.

MORE VARIATIONS ON A THEME

A casual glance at Anna's second, larger SCA shows the members are in very unequal positions due to the luck of the draw. Anna got her funds first, so she received a large loan. Zoca received her funds last, so she didn't get any loan. In addition, Zoca took the greatest risk that all members might not pay throughout the cycle and suffered the most from inflation. Fortunately, these inequities can be equalized or turned into extra value for the members to share.

One of the inequities is that participants receive different loan amounts because of their position in the draw. Some SCAs solve this dilemma by bidding out the right to receive the next payment to the members who have not yet received their payments. The money received in the auctions is often shared equally by either all of the members or just the members who have not yet received their payments. This allows the people who need a loan the most at any given time to receive it, while those who need one the least can wait and not pay extra to get a loan until it is their turn. It is not uncommon

for the offer for the first payment in a large SCA to be as much as 20 to 50 percent of the amount of the first payment.

The auction process not only eliminates the unequal benefit of receiving loans early but it more fairly shares the risk of repayment and the effects of inflation. Clearly, those who receive the payments early in the cycle are the most likely to quit making their payments. The two primary safeguards against this are loss of social standing and acquiring a bad reputation so they cannot join future SCAs in the community. Although these are strong incentives to continue making weekly payments, they are not fail-safe. So innovative SCA members have found a way to mitigate the risk. They've also found a solution to the perplexing problem of recruiting trustworthy members. Finding reliable members and ensuring that everyone makes timely payments is quite a task. Having the time and contacts to find enough reliable members for large SCAs is difficult for those who are also working long hours to make a living.

FOUNDERS

In very large SCAs, both repayment and organizational issues can be solved by having a founding member who is responsible for organizing the group, collecting payments, and guaranteeing timely payments. Additionally, a founding member makes it possible for the members to be strangers who don't necessarily live or work in the same location. Equally important, the founder can serve as a community liaison who educates people about the benefits of joining an SCA.

Founders obviously have costs involved with forming and running SCAs. So they may charge fees for their service, which vary in amount according to the time and risk involved. A typical founder fee might be to receive the first payment while not putting in any weekly payments. Under this type of fee structure, the cost of a founder is not justified until the SCA is fairly large. For instance, if the SCA only had four other members, the cost of the founder's fee is about 20 percent, while with 50 other members, it is less than 2 percent.

Some types of founders might be able to form groups for small fees. For example, assume a local grocer is the founding member of a small SCA. Her collecting costs—in terms of time and energy—would be minimal because members come to her store regularly anyway. She knows the creditworthiness of her neighbors and customers, and she has the power to withhold groceries until all payments are made. Since an SCA is a benefit to her community, and consequently to her, the grocer might be willing to form the SCA for a small cash fee. As we will discuss later, missionaries, churches, and charities might similarly choose to be founders for reasons other than financial.

In contrast, assume the founding member is a professional organizer who puts together large SCAs made up of people living in many locations. This is the business of professional organizers, who have high costs and risks, as they no longer personally know members of the group. A professional organizer might charge a high fee, but if it is spread out over many members, the percentage cost could be acceptable. The profit potential for organizing large SCAs is substantial. A few years ago, I was approached to join a group of investors wanting to raise millions of dollars to form a large business that would act as a founding member for thousands of SCAs.

Founders and members must tailor the fee structure to fit each situation. Members of an SCA are typically willing to pay reasonable fees for the valuable services they receive.

RICKSHAW ROSCAS

Perhaps the best book written on SCAs is *The Poor and Their Money*, by Stuart Rutherford. Rutherford tells this story of one of his favorite variations on SCAs:

> Poor men driven from villages by poverty come to Dhaka where the only work they can get is to hire a rickshaw, for say 25 taka a day (about $0.63) and hope to earn a daily profit of, say, 80 taka (about $2). In the 1980s such men—illiterate and new to the city, and without any help from NGOs or other sources—devised a standard ROSCA system which has worked to the advantage of many thousands of them. Groups of them get together and agree to contribute 25 taka a day to a kitty which is held, for the time being, by a trusted outsider (often the keeper of the stall where they take their tea at the day's end). Every ten days or so there is enough in the kitty to buy one new rickshaw, and that rickshaw is distributed by lottery to one of the members. The process continues until everyone has his own rickshaw. They have learnt how to adjust the number of members, the daily contribution, and the interval between rounds, to best suit their cash-flow and the price of a rickshaw. But one of the finest innovations is the rule that once a member has "won" his rickshaw in a draw, he must from then on contribute *double* each day.[1]

Over time and in other countries, the amounts of money change, and variations on the SCA abound. However, in all cases, SCAs offer men and women in poverty a method to use their money to generate new opportunities to earn and save.

THE SKY IS THE LIMIT

The basic operations of SCAs are fairly simple, and they have multiple advantages and few disadvantages. As we have seen, with their immense creativity, those living in poverty have found ways to mitigate most of the disadvantages. One disadvantage is the inflexibility that each SCA member has to make the same payment every week for the same number of weeks even though individual opportunities and needs may vary greatly. There are two well-known solutions to this dilemma.

One simple way around this is for people to join more than one SCA. For instance, a woman might join one SCA that ends at the time school fees are due, another ending near the time when she needs to buy seed for planting, and a third providing her with $10 at the end of every month. One of my acquaintances told me that his mother lives in Belize and is continually a member of at least five SCAs.

Another solution is to modify the SCA so it works more like the credit unions so popular in the United States. Introducing the concept of record keeping allows members to pool their savings and make loans to themselves in variable amounts. Since there are few overhead costs, the pool of savings grows quickly as the borrowers pay fees and interest. Because funds accumulate over time, rather than rotating to a different member each meeting, these groups are known as accumulating savings and credit associations, or ASCAs. Limits on the size of the loans, terms of repayment, and amounts of interest and fees are set by the members or their elected leaders. It is in everybody's self-interest to make the terms such that there is a balance between the loans desired and the savings available. If the agreement is for the group to exist for a long time, the members might regularly distribute the interest payments to themselves as dividends. If the agreement is for the group to exist for a short time, the members might split the total pool equally among themselves on the last day. In either case, this arrangement is more able to meet the variable needs of both savers and borrowers than a simple SCA, but it is more complicated to run.

I once met with the representatives of a Russian cooperative who ran an organization like this. They paid their members a 25 percent annual interest rate on savings but charged their members 40 percent for loans. At those two rates, they were able to entice members to save but were still able to loan out all the money they wanted.

REPUBLIC OF CONGO

FINALLY, A SOLUTION FOR RURAL AREAS

Although SCAs work well in urban areas, a special advantage of SCAs is their ability to aid those in areas of low population density. People living in poverty in rural areas are almost completely without access to formal financial services, because it is often cost prohibitive for banks and large organizations to reach so far outside high-density urban and suburban centers. Since there is little room in rural SCAs for businesses to make big profits, it is up to government organizations and nonprofit organizations to find a way to share the idea if it is to have a major impact on the world.

One major advocate of church-based SCAs is the Chalmers Center, which originally grew out of Covenant College in Georgia. Chalmers has trained churches and ministries in over 100 countries around the world to use SCAs as part of a holistic ministry to those in poverty. As a result of an early Chalmers training held between 2005-2007 in East Africa, the Anglican Church in Rwanda invited HOPE International to begin forming SCAs among its members, which we'll discuss more in Chapter 11.

An estimated 9 million people are members of SCAs worldwide.[2] Their popularity has grown in recent years, with the number of members exploding from 1.5 to 7 million between 2009-2013.[3] Among U.S.-based institutions, CARE, Catholic Relief Services, Plan International, World Vision, World Relief, and Saving for Change (a collaboration between Oxfam America and Freedom from Hunger) have embraced this approach and have launched locally adapted versions of the model in many countries. Some SCAs in Latin America have grown so large that they can lend people money to buy cars and houses. In a taxicab in New York City, I learned that SCAs are active in the United States. My driver said he thought at least half of all cab drivers participate in a similar model.

SCAs are an effective way for people in poverty to grab brass rings by empowering themselves to save money and obtain loans. While SCAs are simple to administer and allow groups to set their own fees, they do lack the flexibility to meet certain needs, as loans are limited by the amount of money groups have saved, as well as the higher interest rates and short repayment periods that groups often set for themselves. To address these problems—and to bring even more essential financial services to those who need them—a Bangladeshi economics professor pioneered a different type of microenterprise development.

7

Microfinance Goes Mainstream

(PHIL)

On December 10, 2006, Muhammad Yunus was awarded the Nobel Peace Prize for his historic work with microfinance. When his name as winner was announced in October 2006, millions of people around the world had the same reaction: "Who is Muhammad Yunus, and what is microfinance?"

Yunus was the dean of the economics department at Chittagong University in Bangladesh. Unlike some of his academic peers, he never lost his compassion for men and women on the margins. Passing a low-income neighborhood every day on his way to work, he began thinking of creative ways he could help unlock the entrepreneurial spirit and enterprising potential of the people he saw. He began to roam through villages, asking people in poverty about their sources of income and access to credit. What he learned was daunting—without access to loans at traditional banks (both for economic and geographic reasons), families were often trapped in harsh repayment cycles with local loan sharks who charged as much as 20 percent interest per day.

Rather than make the common assumption that people in poverty will not willingly repay loans, Yunus began thinking of a creative way for them to receive loans so they could prove themselves to be safe credit recipients.

Rather than assume that administrative costs for managing countless small loans would be prohibitively expensive, Yunus visualized ways to reduce costs to a minimum. Instead of being defeated by the lack of collateral or legal standing among those he desired to serve, he worked on a loan design that would overcome those problems. In the end, he had to answer a single basic question: "How can I make sure that those living in poverty will pay me back?"

To test his theories, Yunus decided four decades ago to personally invest $27 in small loans to help a group of women break free from loan sharks and increase their incomes by improving their small businesses. Unlike his peers, Yunus was not surprised when all the women repaid their loans. These loans were the beginning of Grameen Bank, a Bangladeshi institution that is 94 percent owned by its borrowers and has now loaned over $19 billion.

Yunus' economic theories are the basis for modern microfinance. He continues to be an outspoken advocate of microfinance and is perhaps one of the most influential individuals in international development. It is not an

UKRAINE

overstatement to say that he and other microfinance pioneers changed the trajectory of global economic development.

Thomas Edison said, "Genius is 1 percent inspiration and 99 percent perspiration." The inspiration of Yunus and other microfinance pioneers was finding a way to collect loans made to people without collateral. The perspiration came from raising money and experimenting with different loan techniques until their ideas were proven correct. As a result of their genius, hundreds of millions of people have already benefited.

MICROFINANCE

Microfinance is defined as providing financial services, such as small loans, to people in poverty so they can increase their income and decrease their vulnerability to unforeseen circumstances. Microfinance has been successful around the world. It works for one simple and indisputable reason—the vast majority of its clients are willing and able to lift themselves from poverty if given an opportunity.

Edith took advantage of her opportunity. Living in Bujumbura, the capital of Burundi, she used to sell a few vegetables from a small table in front of her home. But that table didn't bring in enough income for her to contribute to her family: "I used to send my children to their father for any of their needs, particularly school-related fees. ... If my husband left the house without giving me money for salt, then until he returned, I could not find anywhere else to get that small amount of money." With an initial $30 loan from Turame Community Finance, a local, Christ-centered microfinance institution, Edith diversified the vegetables she sold. As she paid back her loans and accessed larger ones, Edith expanded to sell non-perishable items like coal. Now she has a stand at the local market, where she sells a variety of additional staples like cassava and cooking oil. She appreciates the ability to contribute to her family, sharing, "My children can testify of the value that Turame brought to our family."

WHY LOANS?

In developing countries, a large number of people make their living through small businesses that run on a cash basis. Imagine running such a small business. All your transactions are cash, and you barely have enough money to pay the bills at the end of each day. You must pay the highest prices for your inventory and equipment because you can buy only in small quantities from a limited number of sellers. Your customers have access to only a small amount of inventory, which you have to sell at low prices because you don't have the margin to refuse any reasonable offer. Your perishable goods decay quickly because you lack the equipment or space to preserve them. You travel to suppliers frequently, limiting the time you can spend at your business and adding significant travel costs. At the end of every day, you take your money and inventory home, where you have no safe place to protect it from theft or the fires and water damage to which flimsy shelters are so susceptible. This is the reality of most small business owners in the developing world; it is untenable from a financial perspective. These business owners are always clinging to the edge of the cliff.

With small loans effectively invested, however, entrepreneurs in poverty have found they can improve their businesses and increase their incomes. They can buy in bulk, travel less frequently to buy inventory, stock more goods, offer services needed in their communities, and buy equipment to reduce labor costs and increase output. None of these basic business strategies are difficult to understand or execute if capital is available—but they are impossible otherwise.

WHO MAKES THE LOANS?

Microfinance institutions (MFIs) provide access to loans using capital from outside sources such as donors or commercial lenders. Until the late 1990s, most MFIs were nonprofit organizations that used donor contributions to make loans. By 2008, there were thousands of MFIs, many of which were operated as for-profit organizations. MFIs range in size from tiny organizations with a few thousand dollars making loans in a single community to huge networks with hundreds of millions of dollars making loans in many countries.

The only contact many people ever have with an MFI is through a loan officer. Unlike U.S. banks, where loan officers sit behind desks and award loans to the best applicants, MFI loan officers typically travel by foot, bike, or motorcycle to villages,

INDIA

where they meet people, organize borrower groups, and make and collect loans.

As one review of MFIs observed, "The loan officer makes or breaks borrowers' experiences. In addition to being the face of the MFI, the loan officer can give clients the information and support they need to thrive in business and at home. During early discussions of the loan process, the loan officer can help determine the appropriate loan amount and how the client will earn enough to repay."[1]

We will go into greater detail about MFIs and loan officers, but first let's look at the types of loans they make and collect.

ABOUT THE LOANS

The sizes of these loans vary from country to country and from MFI to MFI, but the first loan made to an entrepreneur is generally between one-quarter and one-third of their country's average annual income. In very low-income countries, a first loan might be $100, while in middle-income countries, it might be $1,000. If the borrower pays back a loan on time, she typically qualifies for a follow-up loan of a bigger size.

A routine term for a small loan is six months, with payments made every week or two. For instance, a $100 loan might have weekly payments of $4 to $5. As the MFI collects these payments, it recoups money it can use to make new loans. With six-month loans, an MFI can recycle money twice in one year. However, because payments are made weekly, it is theoretically possible for an MFI to recycle money up to four times a year, every year. This is a distinct advantage of microfinance over typical charities that use money only once.

Like many people, when I first learned about microfinance, I assumed repayment rates would be low. Surely many borrowers would simply fail to live up to their end of the bargain. However, I was stunned to learn that the repayment rate of most well-run MFIs is greater than 95 percent and often tops 98 percent. For instance, HOPE International's five-year repayment rate is currently 98 percent. Although this statistic sounds outlandishly high to Americans (7.7 percent of whose credit card accounts were over 90 days overdue in 2015[2]), this is actually a rather typical repayment rate for MFIs around the world.

How did MFIs solve one of the most intractable problems of any lender—making certain people pay back their loans?

Yunus and other microfinance pioneers understood people in poverty lack collateral to secure their loans; therefore, any loans would have to be unsecured "signature" loans that are typically very risky. They found the solution to this problem in the concept of a social guarantee. Microfinance pioneers formed borrower groups of between six and eight women. Each woman received her own loan, but each member of the group cross guaranteed the loans of all the other group members. In other words, if a woman does not make a payment for her loan, the other members of her group have to make it for her. These cross guarantees are the primary reason most efficient MFIs have high repayment rates. Borrowers know it is in their best interest to support and discipline each other at business and at home. This system of accountability and support helps build strong borrowing groups and communities that have a common goal: to lift their families and communities out of poverty.

Enforcement of the cross guarantee is best for everybody in the long term. I once sat in a meeting where one of the borrowers did not show up to make her payment. The loan officer refused to end the meeting until the payment was made. Eventually one of the women left to find the absent borrower and

DOMINICAN REPUBLIC

bring her to the meeting, where she made her payment. I assure you that the other borrowers were unhappy about wasting an hour of their time in the hot sun, and they let her know it.

Another reason for high repayment rates is that borrowers who repay on time qualify for larger follow-up loans with which they can continue to grow their businesses and profits. This is a strong incentive to repay on time. Each borrower understands that the opportunity to access affordable capital is not one they can afford to squander. There is power in a mother who wants to provide for her family. If this is her opportunity to expand her business and provide school fees and better nutrition for her family, she will move heaven and earth to repay her loan on time.

Since borrowers cross guarantee loans, most MFIs require regular meetings so that payments are made in front of the entire group and to offer additional training. In later chapters, we'll discuss how these regular meetings are another way in which borrowers can build their communities and receive other important benefits.

WHAT ARE THE INTEREST RATES?

After fees are included, the average annual interest rates on microfinance loans typically range between 12 and 60 percent. To put it in different terms, I typically think of the annual interest rates as being between 10 and 25 percent plus the rate of inflation for the country involved. Although these rates seem high, they are similar to the rates charged for unsecured signature loans in the United States. However, since the rates initially seem outlandishly high to most people, and since high interest rates are a primary source of criticism of microfinance, let's delve more into the reasons behind them.

A base assumption of microfinance is that an MFI should become self-sufficient so it can survive and service its customers for the long term. Although experts have different terms for levels of self-sufficiency, a self-sustaining MFI would have enough interest income to pay for inflation, defaults, and operational overhead. If the MFI does not have enough interest income to cover these costs, it has to raise more money, take money out of its loan base, or reduce its services.

Inflation is often the hardest factor to consider. It's not an obvious expense that shows up on the income statement or balance sheet. However, if its loan base is not increasing by the rate of inflation, the MFI is going backwards. One statistic that can be misleading is the inflation rates of different countries as given by various government agencies. Bluntly, many governments, especially in developing countries, publish inaccurate statistics. I once met with some wealthy borrowers living in Russia who were able to borrow money from a state-controlled bank at 10 percent per year because the government wanted to have an interest rate policy consistent with a low inflation rate. These borrowers took the money back to their community, where they deposited it as savings in a locally owned credit union for a rate of 25 percent per year. The citizens knew the true inflation rate was much higher than the government pretended and profited by acting in accordance with reality.

DOMINICAN REPUBLIC

As mentioned earlier, loan defaults are generally low in MFIs, but even so, the income from interest must cover the defaults or the MFI's capital base is reduced.

Operational overhead includes the cost of loan officers, back office people, computers, travel, and other direct costs in the field. Even though these costs in many countries are low compared to the United States, they are still high when compared to the size of most MFI loan portfolios. Although tiny loans are involved, the entire loan process must be run with high operational precision. If the payment is only $1, it must be recorded the same as if it were a $100,000 payment. Another reason for high operational costs is that most MFIs provide other services—such as training and insurance—that are built into the cost of the loan. Furthermore, since loan officers travel to the clients, the clients don't need to spend the time and money traveling to cities where loans might be available. The travel costs of loan officers who trek to distant towns and villages are reimbursed indirectly through higher interest rates.

Borrowers are typically much more concerned about having access to loans than they are about high interest rates. In most cases, they have no other access to loans, and if they do, the interest rates from their other options are higher than from microfinance institutions.

The MFI loan interest rate is not the crucial component in success or failure. Consider the woman who borrows $50 and pays it off weekly over six months. Even at an average interest rate of 50 percent per year, she only pays a little more than $6 in interest ($50 x 50 percent interest x ¼ year average outstanding). If she wisely invests the $50 in her business, she very likely will make far more than that in net income.

It is crucial for an MFI to charge interest rates that allow it to become self-sustaining in the long term so that it can continue to service its community. A financially solvent MFI means the community can count on having access to loans and other financial services, rather than relying on loan sharks as their only source of capital.

INTEREST RATES ARE ONLY PART OF THE STORY

Many people with ready access to capital do not understand that interest rates are not the whole story when it comes to the real cost of a loan. When I want a loan, I put in an application online or by going to a local bank a couple of miles away. After a short wait, I either get the loan or I don't, depending on my credit rating. The time and cost of getting a loan are minimal. It's not that way for people living in poverty in developing countries.

I once saw a confidential government report on farm loans in an Asian country. The report explained how people chose among their three borrowing options: local moneylenders at rates far exceeding 100 percent per year, government-sponsored MFIs with far lower interest rates, or government agencies that might not charge any interest at all. The farmers took into account many factors other than the interest rates, such as how far they had to travel to make the loan request, the cost of traveling, the time required to get loan approval, the likelihood of getting loan approval, the cost of bribes, and if another loan might be needed in the future. The report concluded that after all the relevant cost factors were taken into account, the farmers were correct to make use of all three loan options, depending on the specific circumstances at the time. These farmers understood there are many costs and considerations when choosing which loan option best suited their needs.

MICROFINANCE AND WOMEN

The vast majority of small loans—around 75 percent worldwide[3]—are made to women. Men are more likely to be employed if there are jobs in the area, while women are more likely to run small household businesses. At the same time, women often have less access to financial services; around the world, they are 15 percent less likely to have a bank account than men.[4] Women are typically more reliable in repaying loans, as they tend to shoulder the burden

BURUNDI

of family support more than men. A Rwandan proverb states, "A woman is the heart of the home." Helping a woman helps her entire household.

Francia Leonardo is a beauty salon owner in the Dominican Republic. She used her first loan from Esperanza International to purchase a generator, allowing her to keep her business open during frequent power outages. A few years after she started with Esperanza, her husband left her when she was pregnant with their fifth child. Though this was a difficult time for Francia, it ultimately led her to a relationship with Christ, thanks largely to her relationship with her loan officer. Francia was also able to meet the additional financial challenges of being a single mother of five children, taking out loans to invest in her business and increase her income. Francia is passionate about her children's education and is currently helping her oldest daughter pay for college.

RESPONSIBLE USE OF CREDIT

One of the most important functions of an MFI is to educate its borrowers and potential borrowers about the responsible use of credit. In most cases, MFIs require their borrowers to use loans for a single purpose—to increase their incomes.

If borrowers cannot increase their income, it is unlikely they will be able to repay their loans, which is bad for everyone. MFIs take precautions to ensure that borrowers are not using their loans to repay other loans or to purchase consumer goods. They also don't allow spouses or other relatives to confiscate the loan. To maximize the impact of credit, the majority of the loan *must* be used to increase income.

DOES MICROFINANCE WORK?

There have been a limited number of impact assessment studies about microfinance, which we discuss in Chapter 9, but the most powerful way of understanding the impact of microfinance is to see it in action. I became a believer when I walked by a bus stop in a small town in Ukraine.

I watched the bus unload only a few people but an immense number of boxes. I turned to my microfinance loan officer "guide" and asked about the situation. He said, "The people getting off the bus are mostly our clients. They previously took small amounts of money to the neighboring city, bought a few goods, and came back to sell them that day. Depending on how much they sold, they went back the next day for replacement inventory. Now that they have more money from loans, they only go once a week, have more time to sell their goods, buy in bulk at reduced prices, and even buy goods to resell to other vendors. They have reduced transportation costs, pay less for their inventory, have a better selection of inventory, and even make money off the other vendors."

It all fell into place for me. We intuitively understand that effective mobilization of capital is required for countries to grow economically, and it's no less true for the millions of small businesses that make up a large part of many developing economies. Access to capital is a key ingredient allowing people in poverty to make better business choices. Microfinance simply makes good sense. Two important corollary points are worth noting:

- Borrowers highly value their loans and usually try to get one or more follow-up loans. This means borrowers typically believe they are reaping substantial benefits from the loans—a powerful testament to the potential benefits of this system.

- The penalty exacted by an MFI is less menacing than the threat of physical violence from the local loan shark. If a loan is not paid back to a microfinance institution, the penalties are loss of respect in the community, the ineligibility for follow-up loans, small fees, and the costs to co-guarantors who are required to pay back the loan. Those are significant costs to be sure, yet they pale in comparison to harsh physical harm or a child being handed over for slave labor.

ASPECTS OF SCALE

Microfinance institutions can benefit from operating at larger scales. One advantage of organizing a sophisticated microfinance infrastructure is that it can be replicated rather easily. It is possible for one MFI to have central offices in many countries and for those central offices to service branch offices and community banks in thousands of locations. Some MFI networks—such as Accion International, FINCA International, VisionFund, Women's World Banking, and HOPE International—serve hundreds of thousands or millions of borrowers around the world.

Another potential benefit of size is that the percentage of the cost of overhead compared to income shrinks as organizations grow. When this happens, the organization can use more of its resources to help people in poverty. Larger MFIs are also more easily able to offer other financial services, such as savings accounts and insurance. As noted in previous chapters, families in poverty often value the opportunity to save much more than the opportunity to borrow.

In many countries, an MFI must be a regulated financial entity before borrowers are allowed to have savings accounts. The process of becoming regulated is usually expensive and time consuming. An MFI is often required to have several million dollars in capital and become a for-profit entity instead of a nonprofit entity. However, savings accounts not only benefit the borrowers, they offer a huge benefit to the MFI. Once an MFI is able to offer savings accounts, it typically gains the right to use the savings accounts as a source of loan funds to other borrowers. Consequently, many MFIs value this new source of lending capital because it keeps them from having to raise money from unpredictable donors or borrow from commercial sources.

MALAWI

TRENDS AND EVENTS

Successful and expanding MFIs are primarily driven by the desire to lend increasing amounts of money and to provide better services. Sometimes these desires work together and sometimes they are in conflict. Note the paradoxes when we look at the possible sources of loan capital for MFIs:

Donors

Donors want MFIs to have low overhead rates and provide many services to people in poverty. However, low overhead rates typically mean the MFI needs to grow larger, spend more money raising money, and reduce the number of services it offers. Individual donors are hard to find and hard to count on for the long term. This makes it difficult for a growing MFI to count on donor funds.

Profits

An MFI can generate additional money to lend by having profit. However, profits often improve by increasing interest rates and/or reducing services to borrowers.

Commercial Sources

An MFI can increase the size of its loan portfolio by borrowing money from outside commercial sources. These sources might include commercial banks, professional investors, foundations, and mutual funds. These commercial sources are, in turn, driven by the need to be repaid and make a profit, so they tend to push MFIs to increase interest rates and reduce services. Although there is a cost to MFIs to have this money—and it involves risk for MFIs borrowing in one currency and lending in another—it is often easier and cheaper to access than donor money and can usually be accessed in very large amounts.

The history of microfinance demonstrates how these trends play out:

- In 2007, the Mexican microfinance group Banco Compartamos completed an initial public offering, selling 30 percent ownership of the bank. The existing investors received $450 million. Based on its extremely high profit margins, this for-profit organization commanded a market value of $1.4 billion. While some lauded its success, others berated the shareholders for being greedy and taking advantage of those who had no other source for loans.

- Fonkoze, an MFI located in Haiti, starts two community banks a month at a cost of $50,000 each. On average, each community bank is self-sufficient after one year and can begin repaying its loan capitalization. Fonkoze borrowed money in order to start a large number of these banks. Without the ability to borrow money, Fonkoze would have to grow at a much slower pace.

- UPS awarded $1 million to three microfinance organizations, announcing, "There could be no better way to celebrate founder Jim Casey's entrepreneurial spirit than to award grants to foster opportunities for entrepreneurs around the world."[5]

Prior to these types of funding becoming available, funding from individual donors was the primary source of MFI capitalization.

In the end, the beneficiaries of microfinance are the clients, such as Helène Koutika in the Republic of Congo. When she first started with HOPE Congo, Helène sold meat from a couple of tables in the market. She used loans to increase her stock of fresh meat, and as she faithfully repaid her loans and took out larger ones, she purchased a refrigerator and eventually opened her own store. With her own shop, Helène has expanded to offer a variety of vegetables, dried goods, oil, and drinks. She employs one of her daughters, passing on what she's learned about running a successful business. Helène hopes to one day purchase a generator to better support her freezers and open a second shop.

Microfinance has become a well-accepted technique to reduce poverty in developing countries around the world. To summarize, microfinance allows the following:

- Outside capital flows into low-income communities, stimulating additional economic activity.

- Funds are recycled to other borrowers within the community, maximizing the impact of funds.

- Programs can be replicated to serve many borrowers.

Many MFIs and donors recognize that the "theme" of microfinance described in this chapter is just the beginning—and that it becomes more powerful when paired with other services.

MOLDOVA

8

Exploring Variations

(PETER)

When you sing "Twinkle, Twinkle, Little Star" to your child at bedtime, you might be unaware that this simple melody was the basis for a Mozart piano masterpiece. In "Variations on *Ah vous dirai-je, Maman*," Mozart takes a simple theme and creates 12 complex and beautiful variations that challenge accomplished pianists. In a similar way, we have described the core methodologies of savings and credit associations and microfinance institutions and their "theme" of unlocking productivity through savings and small loans. But this is just the beginning. This chapter shows the incredible variations possible through microenterprise development.

Microfinance institutions currently reach over 211 million entrepreneurs and their families.[1] This is an extensive network. Innovators recognize that this vast distribution channel has the capacity to provide many other valuable services to families in poverty. If such services can be provided with little extra effort or cost, then why not do so? This is the vision of "microfinance plus": to provide a holistic range of services—insurance, counseling, training, immunizations, and so forth—to clients through the basic framework of microenterprise development.

When an MFI decides to add a product or service to help its clients, it typically costs a small amount to do so. The MFI already has in place the necessary resources to make and collect small loans. It already has personnel who are respected and have an implied authority in their borrowers' lives. Because of this, many charities and nonprofit organizations are already working with MFIs, giving them products or services cheaply or at no cost because they know MFIs can distribute the products and help ensure their acceptance.

Variations on the theme of microenterprise development are pushing the boundaries—with several innovative "products" reaching street dwellers, youth, and people in prostitution.

CELL PHONES

One of the first successes in expanding the boundaries within microfinance was orchestrated by Muhammad Yunus and Iqbal Qadir in Bangladesh with Grameen Phone. In 1995, Grameen Bank had already established a network of more than 2 million entrepreneurs spread over 35,000 villages and was anxious to see what it could accomplish next. Yunus and Qadir recognized that knowing the current market price for commodities could greatly enhance the bargaining power of farmers in poverty, and that a three-minute phone call could save hours for a merchandiser who needs to know if her goods have arrived in a nearby city. Propelled by the communications revolution of the 1990s, they realized villagers around the world could access a wealth of information via cell phones if only they had access. Select Grameen clients received a loan to purchase a cell phone. In an environment where there were very few phones and financially there was no way each villager could afford a phone of her own, the "cell phone ladies" became a key part of the community's commercial activity while also growing a thriving small business. Think of it as the Bangladeshi version of the pay phones that were commonly seen at gas stations, airports, and restaurants in our country until everyone had their own cell phone.

Others have followed Grameen Phone's example. Urwego in Rwanda began working with the Grameen Foundation in 2006 to provide "phone loans" to existing clients located in rural areas. Clients used these loans to purchase a village phone kit from Mobile Telephone Networks (MTN) that included a cable and extended antenna to be placed in a tall tree or pole in the village, as well as an earpiece and a car battery for charging the phone. Marie-Claire Ayurwanda was one of the entrepreneurs who benefitted from this innovative partnership. A client of Urwego, she initially received a loan to open a small restaurant she called *Isimbi*. She took an additional loan to purchase the phone kit and repaid the loan in only five months. With the phone kit, she sold approximately 30 minutes of airtime per day to her community, providing about $12 of profit each week.[2]

With growing numbers of Rwandans owning cell phones—over 78 percent of the population in 2016[3]—Urwego has continued adapting in creative ways, now offering banking services through mobile phones. Called mHose—*hose* is the Kinyarwanda word for "everywhere"—this system allows clients to make financial transactions over their mobile phones and at participating businesses. Using their phones, clients can access a range of services,

RWANDA

from viewing their savings account balance to receiving and repaying loans to paying utility bills. This provides greater convenience for clients and reduces cash-related risks for loan officers, who no longer have to travel with large amounts of money.

MICRO-INSURANCE

According to the U.S. Census Bureau's 2014 Health Insurance Coverage Report, 33 million U.S. citizens live without insurance.[4] Lack of health care is a serious *problem* in the U.S.; it is a *crisis* in many parts of the world. I have never found an individual living anywhere near the poverty line who had any formal insurance unless it was through an MFI. Insurance is a luxury that most people in poverty cannot afford.

While companies like Allianz AG and State Farm Insurance Companies span the globe, their services seldom (if ever) reach those living in poverty and on the margins in the developing world. But so what? How important *is* insurance? From a business standpoint, would families in poverty even be willing to pay for insurance if it were available?

For families below the poverty line, health insurance is actually of critical importance because it provides some protection from emergencies. Instead of a broken leg and subsequent infection pushing a person into destitution, insurance could allow a trip to the city for a clean cast and a pair of crutches. The collective microfinance network provides a way to cost-effectively provide insurance to those living in deepest poverty in remote parts of the world.

In February 2008, the Bill and Melinda Gates Foundation awarded a $24.2 million grant to Opportunity International's subsidiary, the Micro Insurance Agency (MIA), to significantly expand its insurance products to those living in poverty in Africa, Asia, and Latin America. Now known as MicroEnsure, this organization serves 40 million people in 20 countries, with health insurance premiums as low as $3-$5 per year. This price and delivery mechanism makes insurance affordable for its clients, 85 percent of whom had never had an insurance product before.[5]

Micro-insurance includes a range of products that can help those in poverty manage economic hardship, such as flooding, drought, hospitalization, or a death in the family. Workers in the developing world are more likely to experience hardship that can trap them in lifelong poverty, yet they are less likely to have any type of insurance.

On the ground, such programs are affordable and convenient. Mara, a 31-year-old mother of four, lives in East Timor. Mara pays 5 percent of her loan amount as payment for her insurance premium. This payment is easily covered through her increased business income. She is glad to make the payment because it means that she and her children have regular access to preventive health and even dental services. More important, however, Mara knows that in the event of an emergency, insurance will protect her family from disaster. A microloan gives Mara daily hope and income, while micro-insurance piggybacked on that loan gives her daily peace of mind about her family's health and financial future.

LIFE SKILLS EDUCATION

This morning when I was eating Cheerios with my daughter, I studied the back of the box. When I was growing up, the backs of cereal boxes were the place for brightly colored matching games, mazes, and interesting facts about the world. Now this space is used for something very different—advertising. And not advertising for other General Mills cereals, either, but for Pampers Cruisers. The marketing team at Pampers knows that the back of a Cheerios box is a great way to reach a key demographic—parents of young children.

In a similar way, microfinance institutions have recognized they can reach a captive audience and transmit important messages that could improve the lives of their clientele. Credit with Education, as it is commonly referred to,

PERU

takes advantage of the weekly/biweekly meeting structure of microfinance. A leader in the Credit with Education movement, Freedom from Hunger provides training and technical assistance in health, nutrition, and business and household finance to clients of microfinance institutions around the world.[6]

Microfinance institutions are using their reach to inform clients and their communities about everything from business training to the benefits of breast-feeding, from labor codes to language skills. For example, facilitators with Esperanza do a series of trainings in community bank meetings focused on preventive health—everything from eating well to preventing mosquito-borne illnesses to hygiene. Esperanza also offers female clients screenings for cervical cancer, identifying any potential abnormalities so they can be treated before they become cancerous.

Savings and credit associations also take advantage of regular meetings to provide training. In a small survey conducted by HOPE International among SCA members in Rwanda, Burundi, and Malawi, 99 percent of participants said they desire additional training in topics like farming techniques, business planning, and raising livestock. Even more impressive, 78 percent of respondents said they'd be willing to contribute financially to this training—an indicator of the value they place on this service.

MICRO-PHARMACIES

On one of my trips to Haiti, I either ate some food or drank some water that caused me severe abdominal pain. After two days of living in the bathroom, doctors informed me that I had shigellosis, also known as bacillary dysentery. As soon as we received this diagnosis, my wife ran off to CVS to pick up a prescription for an antibiotic called ciprofloxacin. After popping a few pills, I was back to normal.

When I had this illness, I never once feared for my life. In the United States, it is virtually unheard of to perish from this illness, simply because medicine is readily available. But I was shocked to learn that shigellosis causes more than 1 million deaths each year, mostly in children in the developing world. Mothers and fathers across the globe are mourning the needless loss of their children. The problem is getting affordable medicine to the nearly 3,000 people dying each day. Microfinance institutions can be instrumental in making this happen by leveraging their networks to provide basic health services and access to medicine such as simple antibiotics.

One pioneer in this pursuit to distribute generic medicines to those in need is The HealthStore Foundation. Founded by Scott Hillstrom to address the lack of medical services around the world, The HealthStore Foundation has established a network of micro-pharmacies and clinics whose mission is to provide access to essential medicines to marginalized populations in the developing world. The HealthStore outlets target the most common killer diseases, including malaria, respiratory infections, and dysentery. They also provide health education and prevention services, all within a micro-franchise model called CFWshops (Child & Family Wellness Shops). These franchises receive a supply of high-quality and low-cost drugs, management support, training, and other valuable benefits from HealthStore to ensure the standardization and success of the program.[7]

In this model, the relationship with a microfinance institution helps identify entrepreneurs and expand the message of these health clinics. The reality is that this new access to affordable and life-saving treatments means that when children get sick with shigellosis, they do not die.

MICRO-SCHOOLS

The U.S. Department of Health & Human Services notes that "individuals with less than a high-school education ... are at the greatest risk of becoming poor, despite their work effort."[8] This insight is true in the developing world as well: *Education* is a key to success.

But how do children in poverty access a quality education? Edify was started to answer just that question. Edify is a nonprofit based on the premise that many private schools already exist to serve families in poverty. Started by Christ-following entrepreneurs who have a vision of serving the children of their community, these schools often lack the capital and training needed to expand. Edify partners with these schools to provide training, capital, and education technology to help these entrepreneurs reach even more children in poverty.

Beatrice Bamurange is one such education entrepreneur in Rwanda. "I have a calling to serve the hopeless in Rwanda," she shared, "but did not know where." After visiting a rural village and realizing there was no school to serve the community's children, Beatrice realized this was where God was calling her to serve. She started a small school in someone's home, and she used loans from Urwego to build classrooms and add bathroom facilities. In responding to God's call, she's also inspired others, and three of her friends have now built schools in communities that previously lacked access to education.

RWANDA

CORPORATE PIGGYBACKING

According to joint data from UNICEF, WHO, and the World Bank, nearly 1 in 4 children under the age of 5 suffers from stunted growth, a marker of malnutrition and a harbinger of physical and mental challenges.[9] To combat this crisis, several microfinance institutions have created partnerships that address basic nutritional needs. Once again, Muhammad Yunus in Bangladesh led in innovative and pioneering programs that have impacted other parts of the developing world. He initiated a joint venture with yogurt manufacturer Danone Company to bring healthy daily nutrition to low-income populations in Bangladesh. Known as Grameen Danone Foods, this joint venture is registered as a social business enterprise in which all profits are invested back into the company or the communities it serves. The widespread infrastructure of Grameen Bank allows life-saving products to be quickly disseminated and distributed throughout Bangladesh.[10]

Another example of a corporate partnership occurred between the Center for Community Transformation (CCT) and Pepsi-Cola. Insufficient potable water is a serious issue in Manila, one of the largest cities in the world and home to over 24 million people. Water from the taps is unsafe, and water merchants charge exorbitant prices, forcing people in poverty to drink contaminated water.

To solve this problem, CCT came up with an innovative solution. The center persuaded Pepsi to donate a state-of-the-art water purification system. CCT located the water purification system in the middle of one of the least-served slums in Manila, right next to a water merchant who was charging a day's wage for a day's water. Since then, CCT and Pepsi have built two additional water systems, which are managed as social enterprises by private individuals. While there is a charge for the water, it is a reasonable amount that everyone can afford. The water stations also employ former street dwellers to deliver the water, providing them a sustainable income.

SMALL AND MEDIUM ENTERPRISES

While most microfinance efforts focus on families in poverty, there are other entrepreneurs ready for larger amounts of capital for their small- or medium-size businesses who are unable to obtain traditional loans from conventional banks. Small and medium enterprise (SME) loans are necessary for some entrepreneurs to achieve economies of scale and more rapidly expand a business. These loans help to build a productive middle class and expand employment opportunities. Microfinance institutions are helping these larger entrepreneurs, either by expanding the size of their loans or creating linkages with formal banks and "handing off" entrepreneurs that outgrow the MFI.

For 30-year-old Viorel Lup, starting a chicken farm in his home village of Hinchiris, Romania, is a dream come true. Viorel's family has lived in Hinchiris for generations, but though his relationship with Jesus Christ motivated him to help his community by starting a local business, it proved difficult to get off the ground. He moved to England for much of his 20s, where he worked long days and faithfully set aside money for his future business.

Now that he's returned to Romania, Viorel is using his savings; European Union grant funding; and an SME loan from ROMCOM, HOPE International's partner in Romania, to make his dream a reality. He's built two barns, where he eventually plans to house nearly 40,000 chickens. Viorel hired local people to build his barns and plans to do the same for those who will help care for his chickens. "This is my dream: to help many others. This is the best thing you can do in this world," he shared.

"Small businesses like this are the engine of the economy," says Ionuț Crăciun, a ROMCOM loan officer. While not every entrepreneur achieves this level of success, many like Viorel are ready for larger amounts of capital to continue to capitalize their businesses.

HOUSING

Believing that people can lead more productive, healthy lives if they are not worried about their home collapsing or their belongings becoming wet and moldy, Esperanza International in the Dominican Republic offers home improvement loans to help clients lay cement flooring and construct a watertight roof. Usually larger than most business loans, these loans have a repayment period of one to two years.

Juliana Fermin is an example of a client who has taken out one of these special housing loans. Juliana has operated a salon from her home for many years, allowing her to save money instead of paying rent: "I don't have to pay anyone outside," she shares. "I am investing in my own property." Juliana first took out a loan from Esperanza in 2012, which she used to purchase hair dryers and fix broken equipment. After taking out and repaying several loans, she took out a home loan, using it to build a concrete addition on one side of her house. She plans to move her salon into this addition, giving her more space to diversify by selling clothing to her customers.

AGRICULTURAL FINANCE

In 2002, the Consultative Group to Assist the Poor (CGAP) received funding from the International Fund for Agricultural Development (IFAD) to conduct research on the feasibility of financing small-scale agricultural efforts. They discovered that most microfinance institutions were not meeting the needs of the agricultural sector. The reasons were obvious: Natural disasters or drought can quickly wipe out crops, delivering services to rural areas is expensive, population density is low, economies of scale were difficult to achieve, and loans were so small that it was difficult to cover costs through interest rates. CGAP summarized the findings this way:

> Agricultural finance is notoriously risky. Many farmers need credit to purchase seeds and other inputs, as well as to harvest, process, market and transport their crops. While borrowing on the basis of anticipated crop production might seem logical where collateral assets are few, such loans expose the lender to production and price risk. Natural disaster, a decline in market prices, unexpectedly low yields, the lack of a buyer, or loss due to poor storage conditions are only some of the factors that can result in lower-than-expected revenues. Such a fall in revenues can often lead to high default rates on agricultural loans. The overwhelming failure of state development banks that provided billions of dollars in subsidized agricultural finance to farmers in the 1970s and 1980s, combined with scant rural penetration by risk-averse commercial financial institutions, has led to a widespread dearth of agricultural credit. Yet, new approaches are increasingly being developed to fill this gap in a sustainable and efficient manner.[11]

Despite these daunting challenges to agricultural lending and savings, individuals are showing that there are economic development opportunities within agriculture. HOPE Ukraine, for example, provides loans to entrepreneurs using greenhouses to extend their growing season. Clients use these loans to purchase seeds and fertilizer, build greenhouses, improve heating and refrigeration of their space, and install irrigation systems.

Volodya Grabdovchek owns three large greenhouses, where he grows cucumbers, flowers, tomatoes, and green beans. Each day, he fills his trailer and travels to Lviv, a city in western Ukraine, to sell his flowers. He also sells produce and flowers in his village of Vinogradiv, strengthening the local economy. After investing multiple loans, Volodya's business has flourished. "My family now has a way to earn money," he says. With the profits from his business, Volodya is building a house next to the greenhouses, along with homes for his son and daughter to live in once they are grown. Volodya continues to refer other potential clients to HOPE Ukraine, believing it will help farmers increase their profitability and better steward Ukraine's rich agricultural resources.

ROMANIA

ANIMAL "LOANS"

Heifer International has a proven method of helping farmers around the world. After many years, the organization has learned it must analyze the needs and opportunities of a community before embarking on any project of size since tiny markets are easily oversaturated. After finding the right situation, it selects farmers and trains them in the appropriate ways to raise and care for a particular type of animal. That training may include improving pastureland or building sheds or cages. Heifer International then "loans" the cows, sheep, chickens, or another type of animal to the people it has trained. Rather than walking away and assuming its work is finished, Heifer International monitors the farmers' progress and adjusts as needed. Finally, the farmers "repay" the loans by passing on one or more of the animals' offspring to other farmers in the community.

CLEAN WATER

Pastor Marino Moreta noticed that many children in his community of Fraile Segundo, Dominican Republic, were getting sick from drinking contaminated water. Clean bottled water was available, but at 50-60 pesos ($1.09-$1.31) per 5-gallon jug, it was too expensive for members of his community to buy regularly. In response, Pastor Marino and his church started Vaso de Vida, meaning "glass of life," buying a purifier and equipment to sell clean water to their community. At 20 pesos (44 cents) per 5-gallon jug, the water is much more affordable—and it tests cleaner than more expensive brands.

In March 2014, Vaso de Vida took out an Esperanza water loan, a product specifically designed to help churches provide affordable, clean water to their low-income neighborhoods. Over the course of several loans, Vaso de Vida bought a generator and new filters, as well as a motor for the truck they use to make water deliveries. The ministry now employs seven people and sells

380 jugs of water per day, providing both employment and clean water in their community.

UNDERSERVED POPULATIONS

Microfinance is not just developing new products to assist those living in poverty; it is targeting new and diverse populations left behind by traditional economic assistance. Many people believe that microfinance works only for entrepreneurs who have existing businesses, but this assumption is being challenged. Consider the following examples of innovative microfinance initiatives improving the lives of street dwellers, youth, and people in prostitution.

Street Dwellers

Since Yunus and his Grameen Bank received the Nobel Peace Prize in 2006, microfinance has continued to gain momentum and exposure. However, this increased exposure has also attracted critics who question whether microfinance is reaching those in extreme poverty.

Grameen Bank started a program exclusively for street dwellers called the Struggling Members Program. For Yunus, this was a simple way to test his hypothesis that "all human beings are born entrepreneurs. Some get a chance to unleash that capacity. Some never got the chance, never knew that he or she has that capacity."[12]

Grameen loan officers visit people living on the streets of Bangladesh and explain that a better life than their hand-to-mouth existence is possible. Loan officers explain that these street dwellers could easily turn their begging into a simple business. "As you go from house to house, would you take some merchandise with you—some cookies, some candy, some toys, some sweets?"[13] As people consented and subscribed to specially designed loans— typically no more than $15, repayable without interest, designed as start-up capital for an elementary micro-business—Yunus realized how powerful this mobilized force could be. These de facto door-to-door salespersons, already equipped with sales know-how, were now equipped with the capital to truly profit from their skills rather than simply survive. The incentive to repay these zero-interest loans was the opportunity to receive further loans. By 2008, Grameen Bank had served over 100,000 street dwellers, more than 10,000 of whom had risen from begging into other employment. Of the other 90,000, Yunus likes to claim that they are in the process of closing down their begging division and concentrating on their sales division.[14]

In the Philippines, the Center for Community Transformation (CCT) also found an innovative way to care for those living in deep poverty. *Pulúbi*, or "beggars" in Tagalog, have few opportunities to escape poverty. Manila is a megacity to which people from all over the Philippines move in hopes of finding a job and a better life. Unfortunately, finding sustainable employment is difficult, and many of these hardworking rural transplants are forced to live on the streets. CCT began a visitation ministry to these people and quickly re-

PHILIPPINES

alized their capacity for productive employment. CCT invited a few to come to their offices to work on a temporary basis, and soon these former street dwellers became full-time employees. CCT eventually hired 20 *pulúbi* as full-time employees who were able to leave the streets and live dignified lives.

Since then, CCT's ministry to street dwellers has expanded tremendously. Today, CCT runs a halfway house, where families live for about six months as they prepare to leave the street behind. Children attend school, while adults receive job training in skills like sewing, construction, landscaping, and food production. Members form savings groups, learning the discipline of saving 20 pesos (42 cents) a week and building a reserve in case of emergency. Additionally, participants hear the Word of God and experience discipling relationships with others. Today, hundreds of former street dwellers are gainfully employed, and several children who used to live on the streets are supporting themselves through college. No longer does CCT refer to these hardworking individuals as *pulúbi*, but as *kaibigan*, or friends.

Impoverished individuals caught at the lowest levels of society, when given access to capital, legitimate employment possibilities, and the belief that improvement is possible, are able to live new lives through entrepreneurship.

Youth

As parents join savings and credit associations, they often recognize the value of training their children to save money as well. In Rwanda, 61 percent of the population is under the age of 24, and the median age is just 19. While a majority of HOPE Rwanda's members are adults, there are around 80 savings and credit associations made up of members ranging in age from 12 to 17. Oscar, a 17-year-old who serves as secretary of his group, immediately saw the benefit of forming a savings group: "I had different needs as a child," he shares. One of these needs is education. Sixteen-year-old Vestine uses her savings to buy school supplies. Cecilia, another 16-year-old member, says, "I want to study hard and then get a loan from the group to pay for school fees in a good school." She dreams of using that education to become a doctor.

People in Prostitution

On Valentine's Day in Rwanda, I had an unusual visitor at my home. A prostitute must have known that I was a single American living alone in Kigali, and she came knocking to see if I might be interested in some company. What I *was* interested in was finding a way to help her earn a living without having to sell her body.

The "world's oldest profession" is evidence that some women feel so desperate they will do whatever it takes to survive and provide for their families. If you were living in poverty with children to feed and no prospects for employment, what would you do, particularly when you had a "job" that you knew would pay a sufficient amount? Countless women and children are forced into this form of slavery and often see no way out.

For many women in prostitution, entrepreneurship offers an alternative. If these women know how to sell, why can't it be a product other than their bodies? A Kenyan girl lamented, "I may have to go into prostitution, and then I know I will get HIV and die; I would rather have a real business, but it is not easy."[15]

But what if we could offer hope for the future and a pathway out of poverty? Esperanza identified 15 women (mostly Haitian) who were eager to escape prostitution in Puerto Plata, Dominican Republic, to participate in a program called Forty Days to a New Life. "Someone had to show care for them," notes former Executive Director Carlos Pimentel. "They're in prostitution because of poverty." Esperanza used the curriculum developed in Rick Warren's *The Purpose Driven Life* to lead these women through a 40-day renewal process. Esperanza then introduced small loans, business training, and alternative income sources through entrepreneurship. As a result, many came to know Jesus Christ, most turned their backs on prostitution, and several took a loan from Esperanza to begin a new life.

IT'S TIME TO CHANGE THE WORLD

Sometimes a small discovery has the potential to change the world. Is it possible that microenterprise development will radically reshape the way we address poverty? We now see families in poverty not as objects of charity but as co-participants in the vital work of economic development and global change. Microenterprise development may be the simple, beautiful theme from which variations continue to unfold in wonderful complexity.

Jared Diamond writes in *Guns, Germs, and Steel* that civilizations located at crossroads always develop more rapidly than societies isolated by geographic factors such as rivers and mountains. Our society—indeed our world—now exists at a global crossroads of information and possibility.

Given the flexibility, simplicity, and power of microenterprise development, a dramatic reduction in poverty is a realistic goal.

9

It Can't Be That Good, Can It?

(PETER)

Given the merits of microfinance and savings and credit associations, it would be tempting to see these as *the* tools for ending global poverty, as *the* tools with which the Church can address physical and spiritual needs in every situation. This chapter is meant to temper any unrealistic expectations you might have about microfinance and SCAs. Sometimes exuberance for the observed results of microenterprise development causes its advocates to place that method on too high a pedestal. We must be frank and thoughtful about the shortcomings and limitations of financial services, lest we expect too much of them.[1]

Indeed, in recent years, several articles have come out questioning the impact of small loans on families in poverty. A February 2015 brief from Poverty Action Lab and Innovations for Poverty Action surveyed seven randomized evaluations on the impact of small loans on families in poverty and found only modest results. While they found that families didn't experience over-indebtedness, as some critics had hypothesized, they also didn't find much evidence of increased incomes among participants. What they did find was increased freedom among participants to choose how they invested their money, allowing for greater income smoothing and reducing the many risks inherent in poverty.[2]

Studies like these show the importance of not simply focusing on loans but on providing a variety of services—including the training to use loans wisely and a safe place to save money. They also confirm that financial wealth is only a small part of true flourishing. These studies remind us to take a step back and ask some tough questions.

WHAT DO WE WANT: ERADICATION OR ALLEVIATION?

Some of the most ardent microfinance supporters suggest that it will elimi-nate poverty. Nobel Peace Prize winner Muhammad Yunus shared this vision: "I firmly believe that we can create a poverty-free world if we collectively believe in it. In a poverty-free world, the only place you would be able to see poverty is in the poverty museums."[3] Statements such as this are effec-tive rallying cries, and extreme poverty *has* decreased tremendously, with the number of people living under $1.90 a day dropping from 37 percent in 1990 to less than 10 percent in 2015.[4] However, over-exuberance may raise expectations to an unattainable and unrealistic level, as significant progress will never be the result of only one sector or one specific approach.

Asserting that the goal of these services is poverty *alleviation* is quite dif-ferent from asserting that the goal is poverty *eradication*. Many studies have shown clients increasing and diversifying their income and assets and de-creasing their vulnerability. Even though anecdotal evidence shows it is pos-sible to make large gains, large enough to eradicate that instance of poverty, studies show that the norm is more modest—alleviation. Would a 100 percent increase in an income of $1 per day *eradicate* a family's poverty? Would a 500 percent increase? No, but it would *alleviate* their poverty and provide greater margin against income fluctuations or economic shocks.

A 100 percent increase in income, even from $1 to $2, means a family eats better food, enjoys better health, improves their housing, and has greater confidence and hope for the future. Increased income can radically trans-form local churches as members increase their giving. An increase in income can provide a catalytic boost toward additional improvement—perhaps even permanent escape from poverty. The stories of some clients may not appear dramatic to those in wealthy nations and may not even register as a blip on a country's gross national product (GNP). But for the people earning $1 a day, a second dollar can make a huge difference.

A tempered understanding of the impact of microenterprise development will help ensure new ways of expanding outreach to the millions who have yet to take advantage of this powerful tool while at the same time protect-ing us from the damaging delusion that it will simply erase all of the world's financial problems.

LOANS CAN CAUSE HARM

Unlike other forms of aid, microfinance is not an end product. While a bag of rice is the solution for immediate hunger, microfinance is an *opportunity*, not a total *solution*. When an organization distributes rice in a neighborhood, families enjoy the end benefit of the project: food for the table. With microfinance, the client receives one ingredient, capital, in the broader recipe of income generation. The additional ingredients of time, work, and (often) an existing enterprise must be mixed with the loan in order to achieve the end result. Microfinance is a single step—albeit a very important one—in the process of poverty alleviation.

Not every microfinance client enjoys dramatic success. A percentage fail—a reality in every market economy. Individuals eager to discredit microfinance might dramatize these examples and ignore the benefits obtained by the majority of microfinance clients. Yet even though harm is not the norm (nearly every MFI is focused on seeing their clients succeed), it is instructive to note some of the ways in which microfinance can fail and to remember that such failures represent human lives still trapped in poverty.

Mama Beatrice heard of a promising opportunity in a district outside Kinshasa, the capital of the Democratic Republic of Congo. The rumor mill said that coffee beans could be sold profitably and quickly in this region due to the high cost of transportation and the fluctuating scarcity of certain goods. So, sight unseen, she took out a small loan and invested her capital in coffee beans that she planned to sell outside Kinshasa. Unfortunately, the business rumors were just rumors; it took her months, not days, to sell her stock of coffee beans, and she was barely able to meet her loan payments. Instead of continuing to work at her marginally profitable business as a shopkeeper, using her loan in that business, she ventured into an unsuccessful business based on a rumor and her desire for a quick profit.

Galina and her daughter owned a small business selling clothing in a local market in Ukraine. They had been successful borrowers for two years and proved to be honest and responsible entrepreneurs. Hoping to expand their business, they left the local market and rented a storefront to become a "department store." Using two $2,000 loans, they purchased new winter clothing and expected good sales. Unfortunately, the following winter was unseasonably warm, and the income from their sparse sales covered only part of their rent payments. The landlord confiscated their goods and forced them to leave.

Problems can arise when small loans are misused or when the borrower fails to fully evaluate external risks universal to business. Sometimes, a borrower seems to have no fault yet still fails. In some cases, the borrower is worse off for having taken out a small loan. Borrowing is inherently risky, and despite the best efforts of those involved, a percentage of microfinance ventures will fail.

Realistically, failure to pay back loans is relatively rare among those in poverty. Instead, the client success rate is tremendously high, perhaps because microfinance clients have already been tested and toughened. Before microfinance enters a village, there are few options. Most likely, the only source of capital in town is a loan shark who charges exorbitant rates, yet many are *still* able to operate somewhat profitable businesses. It is no wonder most borrowers embrace microfinance loans and succeed in a new, more nurturing financial environment.

LOANS ARE NOT FOR EVERYONE

Some people are born entrepreneurs, while others seem to lack the drive or talent to use capital effectively. Those who lack entrepreneurial skills might make honest, hardworking employees at factories, hotels, and other income-generating businesses, but very few opportunities for these types of jobs likely exist locally.

When Westerners wonder how it is possible that so many hundreds of thousands of clients are clamoring for business loans, keep in mind that the economy in a developing country is dramatically different than it is in a country like the United States. In many places, formal employment opportunities simply do not exist, even at what we would consider the most basic levels. There are no fast-food restaurants like McDonald's or Taco Bell, no retail chains like Wal-Mart or Target, and few factories that hire manual laborers. White-collar jobs are even scarcer. The complex legal environment and government instability typically found in developing countries discourage foreign investment and compound the shortage of employment opportunities. In these situations, a person who wants to make money has almost no option other than self-employment. A worker's alternative isn't a boring job at a warehouse or collecting unemployment—it is destitution.

Survival is a powerful impetus for individuals to try to sell whatever they can. A woman will bake a few extra loaves of bread to sell on the street, or a man will hawk a leather belt and a pair of shoes. In fact, many microfinance loans finance income-generating activities that supplement, rather than replace, family incomes earned from day labor, agriculture, or other seasonal income. If company jobs were as scarce in the United States as they are in certain parts of Africa—and self-employment were the only option—there is no question that we would be a nation of street vendors and small-scale entrepreneurs, especially if the government did not provide social safety nets.

MICROFINANCE IS BUT ONE PIECE OF DEVELOPMENT

From a development viewpoint, there is a level of need below the threshold that loans can reach. In conflict and disaster situations, grants and emergency care are needed since people can focus on longer-term issues, such as employment, only after their most immediate needs are addressed.

From a financial viewpoint, microfinance provides part of the foundation upon which to build communities, but there also needs to be the next level of small- and medium-size enterprises as well as large corporations. All these

HAITI

work together, and the more a country advances, the greater the opportunities for large-scale investments.

From a spiritual viewpoint, there is a critical need for further training of pastoral staff to teach congregations how to responsibly handle increasing financial resources and how to live out the Gospel in every area of their lives. Economic prosperity will not automatically lead to significant community and church improvement—in fact, the opposite can occur.

Lasting change and development require significant structural changes. Without a system of justice, corrupt leadership like Zimbabwe's President Robert Mugabe can literally destroy all the benefits of small-scale economic development in a day, as he did during Operation Murambatsvina (translated "cleaning up the trash"). Police bulldozed whole communities, including homes and businesses. Suspected to have been a means of punishing political opponents, this operation left 700,000 people without their homes, businesses, or both.[5]

Such injustices must be addressed, along with land reform, access to clean water, educational system improvements, eradication of malaria, and many other critical issues.

MICROFINANCE IS CHANGING

Gatherings for microfinance practitioners have changed dramatically over the past several years—a change easily seen in the participants' shoes. A colleague commented that when he started attending microfinance forums, Birkenstocks were the footwear of choice, but now he's more likely to see polished Salvatore Ferragamo loafers. There is no question that the sector has been professionalized and attracts a host of entrants from the banking and finance world.

One consequence is that there is a growing push in microfinance to focus not only on sustainability and aiding people in poverty but on maximizing profit and shareholder return. If this trend continues, it's possible that distributing other services such as business and health education—key strengths of microfinance—could be cut off in the name of efficiency and profit.

The growth in for-profit MFIs and MFIs seeking funding from commercial sources will fuel the need to achieve low-risk financial returns. Consequently, some MFIs may be more concerned with repayment and profit potential than with changing lives. Although these two goals should not be mutually exclusive, profit-maximizing financial entities could cause MFIs to have only one bottom line—profit.

Technology is rapidly changing microfinance. Loan transactions by ATM cards or by cell phones are now occurring in all parts of the world. These and other advances in technology have the potential to reduce the perceived need for personal contact among borrowers and between loan officers and borrowers. Yet this personal contact—from the perspective of impact, education, and spiritual change—is indispensable.

Given these dynamic changes, MFIs that want to do more than simply deliver access to credit and savings could appear less commercially viable from a financial viewpoint, which could hinder their ability to attract investments.

POWERFUL, NOT PERFECT

Microfinance is not a perfect one-size-fits-all solution, but it *is* an effective tool to help individuals work their way out of poverty and into a better life. No nation has ever developed without investment, savings, and other financial services.

Some critics assert that we shouldn't focus on microfinance because it harms a small number of individuals, but this would be akin to banning penicillin. One out of 5,000 individuals who takes penicillin has a severe allergic reaction, called anaphylaxis, which is fatal unless there is immediate medical intervention. Yet penicillin has saved hundreds of thousands of lives.[6] It would be wrong to consider banning penicillin; instead, we monitor its use to ensure it is properly administered to the right patients in a way that maximizes impact until something better is created. The same holds true for microfinance. Responsible providers regularly monitor the impact and ensure that the staff and group members understand the "warning signs." When an individual is harmed by a small loan, the provider works that much harder to make sure that next time, the loan is successful. To ensure the greatest impact, microfinance programs must guard against focusing exclusively on maximizing profit at the expense of families in poverty.

With microfinance such a potentially powerful tool for fighting poverty, how might the Church become more involved? The answer involves examining the possibilities of fulfilling the missions of the Church, SCAs, and MFIs through a new kind of partnership.

10

Using the Second-Best Distribution System

We hope you are convinced that the Church's mission is to simultaneously alleviate physical and spiritual poverty. How, then, can the Church unite these two critical missions? Can microenterprise development help the Church address both physical and spiritual needs? How might a church-led program differ from a secular one? My quest to answer these questions began when I heard a tirade against the biggest charitable foundation in the world.

"The Bill and Melinda Gates Foundation may be the most important social change agent created in the last 50 years," ranted my friend. "The foundation will very likely cause important vaccines and medicines to be invented which will have the potential to change the lives of hundreds of millions of people. But I believe it will encounter the same point of frustration facing most international charities—how will these medicines be effectively distributed? Can you imagine a truck driving up to a remote African village with a loudspeaker recording of 'Come get your magic medicine! It will make your disease go away!' No, the distribution and acceptance problems will be as costly and difficult to solve as finding the solutions!"

My friend made a lot of sense—I was struck by the difficulty of the distribution problem facing those of us who want to help people living far away in desperate conditions. Although I had seen television scenes of food trucks besieged by individuals looking for food, I had never pondered the logistical problems of distributing food, medicines, and information. It is not just the difficulty of getting goods from the place of origin to distribution points, but the continuing problem of gaining the trust of potential users and educating them in the benefits of unknown products. Without good distribution and acceptance methods, no product or service will be widely used.

Virtually everybody working in international aid has witnessed this problem. One striking example was the time aid workers drove through Goma in the Democratic Republic of Congo after the devastating eruption of Mt. Nyiragongo. These workers indiscriminately tossed protein bars out of their vehicle while a crowd of young Congolese children ran after the vehicle grabbing all they could. Some of the younger children were practically trampled as the faster and more powerful kids hoarded a disproportionate amount. As pandemonium reigned, any onlooker would wonder just how the aid workers would report their "successful" distribution to supervisors and donors in the United States. I wonder the same thing every time I see a similar scene on television.

Even a cursory examination of the acceptance problem reveals the importance of credibility and established relationships. Imagine how you would react if a minor government official or a worker from a charitable organization showed up in your town and insisted that everybody in the community immediately start taking some kind of pills. If you're like me, you would flush your pills down the toilet until you became convinced of their benefit. But if my doctor told me to take the pills, I would take them just because I trust him.

Local residents have to first acquire faith in someone coming to help, or they likely won't believe the benefits of the products or the information. In addition to evaluating the efficacy or utility of products and information, many in poverty will evaluate the person or organization *bringing* the product or information. The people coming to help must establish a relationship with local communities, or they will never be able to communicate the benefits of what they are offering. In the process, both sides probably will have to overcome stereotypes and cultural prejudices.

One of the significant problems that MFIs and SCAs face is the failure of past charity efforts. After all, why should a villager take a loan that must be paid back or save their own money when it is possible another charity might soon appear and simply give away money or goods with no strings attached? And why should a village be expected to believe an organization will treat them fairly when other agencies seem to act in random or destructive ways? Without developing trusted relationships, an MFI will find it difficult to get an opportunity to clearly explain the opportunities and benefits it has to offer. The hopeful message of an SCA program is often poisoned by earlier charity, however well-intentioned that charity effort was at the time.

When a vaccine or food supplement arrives at its destination—even if it makes it *inside* the home of a person in poverty—there is no reason to assume it will be used. People must be educated about benefits, use, and reli-

ability, and that's not only difficult but costly. Throwing money at making better products may not help.

The most likely way to ensure acceptance is through the influence of trusted authority figures in the community or local word of mouth. That isn't easy when so many people in poverty are highly influenced by witch doctors or other local authority figures whose importance would be greatly diminished by outside solutions. Sometimes tradition and cultural norms are wise and reliable; other times they are simply harmful and should be changed. Unfortunately, the history of outsiders coming into communities and making good changes proves not to be any more likely than coming in and making bad changes. Since we Americans are well known for arrogantly believing we know it all, we should take special care to first develop relationships with local community members to make sure we don't make a situation worse because we misunderstood the problem or offered an inappropriate solution.

In 2006, the Chalmers Center signed an agreement with Freedom from Hunger, one of the most respected secular relief and development organizations in the world. This agreement allows Chalmers to integrate biblical worldview messages into extensive curricula for training people in poverty in the areas of small business, household financial management, and health. The Chalmers Center has integrated biblical worldview messages addressing the beliefs of animism into the curricula and adapted these for strategic locations in Africa, Asia, and Latin America. Brian Fikkert, president and founder of the Chalmers Center, tested some of the lessons in the slums of Kampala, Uganda. In one instance, a woman raised her hand and shared, "I'm a witch doctor. After last week's lesson, I went back to church for the first time in twenty years. What do I do now?" That day, she burned her medicines in front of the group and became a follower of Christ. Not only has that witch doctor been personally freed, but her example has greatly enhanced the ability of Fikkert and his colleagues to distribute their information.[1]

As we start examining the distribution and acceptance problems in more detail, it is useful to look at the best distribution system in the world.

BURUNDI

THE BEST DISTRIBUTION SYSTEM

The Church is the best distribution system in the world. This might not be obvious to Americans, even those living in cities with a church building in every neighborhood. Even though large denominations may have tens of millions of members, most of their church congregations are influenced primarily by local leaders. Contrast this to many other churches in the world.

In Africa, there are Anglican bishops who each exercise immense authority over a million or more church members. In Korea, the Yoido Full Gospel Church, led by Young Hoon Lee, has more than 480,000 members.[2] Chinese house church leaders may exercise some level of authority over many millions of members. All of these numbers pale in comparison to Roman Catholicism's Vatican, which exercises authority over 1.2 billion people,[3] or to the 225 million members of the Eastern Orthodox churches.[4]

Pastor and author Rick Warren illustrates this principle through three maps of the Western Province of Rwanda. In the first map, three dots mark the locations of hospitals. The second map identifies the 26 health clinics that serve 650,000 people. The third map identifies the locations of churches—726 dots cover the map. This visual powerfully conveys that the Church has a far greater scope and scale than virtually any other social entity.

Churches around the world are often the most influential distribution systems in their communities. Jobs for Life, a Christ-centered nonprofit working to combat joblessness in the U.S. and around the world, is one organization partnering with this expansive network. Believing that local churches are uniquely poised to help people find meaningful employment in their communities, Jobs for Life equips churches to develop mentoring relationships and provide job training to those in need of work. Trainings include such valuable skills as job searching, networking, integrity, and customer satisfaction.[5]

THE SECOND-BEST DISTRIBUTION SYSTEM

We believe the second-best distribution system for people in poverty around the world is microenterprise development. This approach has already provided capital to hundreds of millions, with billions more to come over the next 20 years. Why is it such a good distribution system? Think about a typical SCA or MFI:

- Its members meet together at regular, often frequent, intervals.

- Its members exercise influence over one another.

- Its members come in contact with many nonmembers on a frequent basis.

- SCA or MFI leaders have a significant amount of actual and implied authority and credibility.

- If an SCA or MFI teams with a local church, it may benefit from some of the influence of that church.

Imagine a community bank meeting held at an open-air church building in the mosquito-infested jungles of Panama. The loan officer collects the weekly payments from 16 borrowers, and then she introduces a nurse to talk about mosquito nets. The local preacher tells them about another church 20 miles away where child deaths have decreased because church members started using mosquito nets. The loan officer then informs the members that she has arranged for another nonprofit to distribute nets for free. She points out that mosquito nets have drastically reduced malaria among her other borrowers who use them regularly. Those influences alone should be enough to get the borrowers to act; however, microfinance makes adoption even more likely. Because of the cross guarantees, every borrower is at financial risk if other borrowers or their family members get malaria. Between the local pastor, a trusted loan officer, and the social demands of microfinance, there will be immense pressure to accept and use mosquito nets.

Community banking methodology also provides opportunities for the MFI to share values and beliefs and to mobilize borrowers toward a particular cause. Grameen Bank leveraged its reach to engage its clients in the political process in Bangladesh. Grameen Bank is committed to making sure all of its members and their families vote in every national election. In the 1996 election, 73 percent of the population turned out to vote, the highest percentage of voters ever recorded there. More women voted in that election than men,

UKRAINE

another voting record and an indicator of the effectiveness of Grameen's efforts. The following year, local elections were held at the village level. This time, Grameen women not only voted but also became candidates. As a result of this social mobilization, more than 2,000 Grameen members, many of them women, were elected into their local governing bodies.

Christ-centered SCAs and MFIs also have the ability to demonstrate and deliver the Gospel message. As a Christ-centered network of MFIs and SCAs, HOPE International has adopted a three-part model to ensure each program is integrating Christ into all its operations: disciple staff members, disciple clients in regular operations, and partner with the local church to make disciples who multiply. While partnering with the Church may look different in Rwanda than it does in Ukraine, for example, HOPE works to make sure each of those three elements is represented in every program.

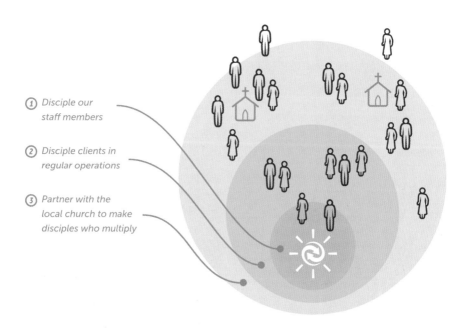

① Disciple our staff members

② Disciple clients in regular operations

③ Partner with the local church to make disciples who multiply

REPUBLIC OF CONGO

In 2008, a research team visited a variety of clients in Rwanda and asked why they chose Urwego over competing MFIs. The answer was clear and consistent among randomly selected respondents: "Because we receive the Word of God!" Staff members are effective in sharing organizational "values and beliefs" that seem to be highly valued and prized by clients and in sharing the Good News of Christ.

THE IMPORTANCE OF RELATIONSHIPS

Loan officers and savings facilitators are the primary point of contact with clients and often become close friends and confidants of those they serve. If the loan officer or savings facilitator is committed to sharing the Gospel, they will have many opportunities to share Bibles, invite clients to a church service, or form a Bible study.

Ramona is a loan officer with Esperanza in the Dominican Republic. She first got to know Esperanza as a client, using loans to purchase supplies for her business selling meat and sausage. But it was the relational aspect of Esperanza's work that made her want to become a loan officer. "I like, truly, to work with people," she shares. Ramona had experience teaching Bible studies and leading Sunday school, and she wanted to use these skills to serve others. Though she knew she wouldn't make as much money, Ramona began praying for an opportunity to work for Esperanza. When her loan officer was promoted to a supervisory role, Ramona had the opportunity to take her place. Now, through her role with Esperanza, Ramona follows her passion of building relationships and sharing her faith with others.

DOUBLE WHAMMY

Microenterprise development is an effective method to help alleviate poverty without causing dependency—and it becomes even more powerful when partnered with the local church and Christ-centered ministries. For many years, HOPE International has adopted a philanthropic dividends policy, in which profitable MFIs in its network donate a certain percentage of their profits to support local children's ministries. This double impact is a primary reason why I am a supporter of HOPE. One example of this is the Tomorrow Clubs ministry, which was founded by HOPE staff members in Ukraine. These clubs meet one day a week after school for about two hours and are led by members of local churches. The children memorize Scripture, sing worship songs, participate in local service projects, and play. Through these clubs, the children and their parents are encouraged to attend church or go to small group meetings. Additionally, the parents become aware of HOPE's microfinance activities that might be of benefit to them. By the spring of 2016, Tomorrow Clubs had expanded into seven other countries in Eastern Europe, and more than 13,000 children were attending these clubs every week.

As members of the body of Christ, we believe the most important "product or service" that can be distributed to anyone is the Gospel. How can the Church partner with MFIs and SCAs to best address physical *and* spiritual needs? We will attempt to answer these questions in the following chapters as we explore microenterprise development in greater depth.

PART III

Joining
the Revolution

PERU

11

Saving with the Church

(PETER)

As we have seen, savings and credit associations (SCAs) have the potential to help those in poverty improve their income, decrease their vulnerability, increase their productivity, and save for life-cycle events such as weddings and school fees. It is important to look at how the local church can advance this powerful concept while fulfilling its other responsibilities.

BENEFITS

Scale

Using SCAs with local churches allows rapid expansion within an existing infrastructure. In many parts of the world, churches are the only entity with such a wide reach. The Most Rev. Emmanuel Kolini is the former head of the Anglican Church in Rwanda and a leader within the worldwide Anglican movement. He founded the Anglican Mission in America, where he continues to serve as the rector of the college of consultors. In addition to his global influence, he continues to focus on those living in poverty in his own country.

Kolini believes that SCAs are vital in carrying out the mandate of the Church to alleviate both spiritual and physical poverty. When Kolini invited me to his humble office in Kigali, he explained his desire that every single congregation in the country would engage in this grassroots strategy: "If every church member could save $50 through SCAs, it would change their lives." Fifty dollars might be enough for me to pay part of my cell phone bill, but for many Rwandans, $50 is the equivalent of a month's salary. It would be the first time these individuals had any sort of safety net, and it would stimulate small-scale economic growth.

Kolini's vision may become reality. Since the Anglican Church began partnering with HOPE International in 2007, its SCA program has grown to serve over 5,000 groups. Additionally, HOPE International has expanded this church-based SCA model to Burundi, Haiti, India, Malawi, Peru, the Philippines, Zambia, and Zimbabwe. As of 2016, HOPE partners with Christian denominations and organizations in these nine countries to serve over 400,000 individuals and their families. These groups save money together, accumulate assets—from mattresses to goats to bicycles—and disburse loans to one another, allowing them to pay school fees for their children, provide more meals for their families, and invest in small businesses. This growth would not have been possible so quickly without the existing framework of local partners.

PERU

Service-Oriented Members

Church-based SCAs can help churches be recognized for their desire to serve and bring healing and wholeness to communities. This is particularly important in places where the image of the Church has suffered. Looking again at the Anglican Church's use of SCAs in post-genocide Rwanda, you can see this is critically important. During the 1994 genocide, about 800,000 individuals were murdered, many of them inside churches where they had fled for safety. There were even a few priests, pastors, and church staff that either directly participated in the killings or stood by as their congregations were slaughtered under church roofs and on church property. As a result, there were Rwandans who vowed never to return to church. In their eyes, the credibility of the Church was destroyed. Thankfully, some of these deep hurts are beginning to heal as churches in Rwanda refocus on serving the community. By helping to organize SCAs, churches are bringing one more element of healing and restoration in Rwanda.

Expanded Outreach

In Malawi, HOPE staff members began asking if the SCA program could be a witness to unreached people groups in the country—groups that do not yet have enough Christ-followers to evangelize their own people. They piloted SCAs among one such group, and as a result, several members came to Christ. I've heard from church leaders in both Malawi and Burundi that this is the first time they've had a tool that effectively brings the Church to their unreached brothers and sisters. Through relationships and meeting real needs, men and women are coming to know Christ—and that is worth celebrating!

Deeper Relationships

God said it first: It is not good for man to be alone. This truth has echoed down through the millennia of human relationships. An Oromo proverb from Ethiopia agrees: "*Kophaan tchaala dansa*" or "Being alone is only good for going to the toilet."[1] For individuals in poverty, isolation makes an already difficult situation nearly impossible.

In the Kayanza Province of Burundi, Jeanette Miburo is the secretary of her savings and credit association, which she heard about through her local church. Since she joined, she has started a business buying and reselling bananas, which she operates with another woman from her group. Jeanette shares, "Thanks to the savings groups, now I am able to give offerings, and my spiritual life has grown up. In addition, I have gained many friends. There is much love among us, and our relationship has been highly strengthened." Whenever group members are hospitalized, the other members collect money for them or help take care of their crops. SCAs are important for those living on the margins because they develop and deepen relationships.

Consider the following account of one SCA in Rwanda composed of members who are blind or have family members who are blind:

> In the beginning, group members saved 3,500 Rwandan francs (RWF), the equivalent of $4.78. They planted a small kitchen garden with leafy and root vegetables for each member. As the group's savings continued to grow to 60,000 RWF ($81.98), they progressed to buying a rabbit and then a pig.

> Alphonse, blind himself, recalled re-educating members that blind people are capable of doing something. Rather than begging, their skills and abilities can be used for gardening, housecleaning, and tending to animals.

> According to Alphonse, members of the group no longer identify with society's labels of "disabled" or "beggar." Now, they have a new name: "savings group members," reflecting their community, belonging, connectedness, and dignity.[2]

RWANDA

Increased Income

In Chisoti, Malawi, Catherine Phiri didn't save money at all before join-ing an SCA. When she first joined in March 2015, she saved 250 kwacha (48 cents) every two weeks. By October, she had quadrupled that amount. She has taken out two loans from her group, for 7,000 kwacha ($13) and 15,000 kwacha ($29), which she used to start businesses selling donuts and buying and reselling common foods like tomatoes and corn. Now she no longer has to rely on relatives to support her but can instead feed her family and pay her children's school fees through her businesses.

TRAINING THROUGH SCAs

Successful SCA programs often include vocational education. This training is critical for entrepreneurs who want to rise out of physical and spiritual poverty.

In Peru, HOPE International's church partner works with a local school to provide baking classes for interested SCA members. When Juvita Cerron joined an SCA, she was a single mother caring for one child with another on the way. Through the acceptance and love of her group, she came to know Christ. "Through joining a savings group," she says, "I found a community that loved me for who I was and reminded me that God loved me too." Juvita had dropped out of college to care for her children, but she participated in the baking training through her group. Now her goal is to save the $200 she needs to purchase an oven and start her own business.

Because of the importance of training, HOPE International partners with the Chalmers Center to train SCA members on group formation, biblical principles, and building relationships, among other topics. SCAs are natural avenues to provide two key elements that break people out of poverty: training and capital.

CHANGED INCOME PLUS CHANGED HEARTS

SCAs are a natural forum for training that goes beyond technical issues. Church-based SCAs emphasize biblical principles about responsibility, relationships, and service while pointing participants toward a loving Savior. This is critically important because, while increasing income is good, it does not automatically lead to a more joy-filled life.

After visiting entrepreneurs in the Philippines, Matt Krol, then board member of Youth With A Mission, observed that "money enables what's in a person's heart." He saw how some individuals seemed to pour their increased profits from their businesses into their families, communities, and churches, while others focused on using their increased capital for selfish purchases.

This is exactly why the Church is uniquely qualified to engage in SCAs. The Church has the moral resources to transform hearts as it helps members improve their savings. This combination is the only way that significant and lasting societal change is possible. Consider the contrasting examples of Florian and Evetta.

Shortly after I arrived in Rwanda, I met Florian. He must have observed that I was looking at houses in the Kimihuhura neighborhood of Kigali, and he approached me and asked if he could be my guard and gardener. He explained that he lost his job and wanted to find a way to provide for his family. In Rwandan society, it is assumed that anyone with even a modest income will provide employment for a guard/gardener. Florian began working with me immediately. He taught me about the local plants and fruits, and I thought we had a friendship that was growing as quickly as the banana plants in the yard. After several months, however, I discovered that when I left, he was entering my house to steal money and valuables from my guests. Worse, he was using his wages and stolen funds to fuel alcohol abuse. I struggled to see how his increased income was actually improving his life, and I recognized that unless Florian's heart was changed, no amount of extra money would make a difference.

The opposite was true for Evetta in Malawi, who shared that though she attended church before joining a savings and credit association, "I didn't want anything to do with God. I used to be a drunkard." She was struck by hearing verses like Romans 12:9: "Love must be sincere. Hate what is evil; cling to what is good" and rededicated herself to the Lord. Now, Evetta says she is more respectful and loving, and she shares her faith with others both inside and outside of the Church. With loans from her SCA, she started buying and reselling tomatoes, and her family is now eating three meals a day instead of two. Though her own crops were damaged by the flooding that occurred in 2015, Evetta gave generously to others who needed food.

These contrasting examples show that increased income alone will not produce the change we long to see. SCAs started in cooperation with a local church can have much greater impact than SCAs working alone. Lasting change can happen when hearts and wallets are transformed simultaneously.

GETTING INVOLVED

SCAs are powerful because they provide individuals living in poverty key tools with which to increase their income—access to a safe place to save and a modest amount of capital. When combined with the local church, SCAs can create lasting physical and spiritual change that flows out of growing relationships between community members. U.S. churches can promote SCAs in ways that build the local church. Given these benefits, perhaps you are ready to learn more or even help support SCA ministries.

The Chalmers Center (*www.chalmers.org*) provides resources for churches eager to get involved. Chalmers trains the Church worldwide in how to minister to families in poverty without creating dependency. Its vision is "for local churches to declare and demonstrate to people who are poor

MALAWI

that Jesus Christ is making all things new." The center advocates for churches to participate in advancing SCAs and supporting microfinance. Chalmers provides resources for both U.S. and international churches, equipping them to walk alongside families living in poverty.

Whenever I am asked about ways for individuals to learn more about microenterprise development, my first response is to point people toward the resources provided by the Chalmers Center. A good starting point is the book *When Helping Hurts*, written by Brian Fikkert and Steve Corbett, which provides a biblical perspective on alleviating poverty without doing harm along the way. In its online portal, Chalmers provides a variety of free resources related to *When Helping Hurts*, as well as its savings curriculum.

It is worthwhile to consider partnering with organizations already experienced with SCAs:

- As previously described, **HOPE International (www. hopeinternational.org)** was invited by the Anglican Church in Rwanda to increase the effectiveness of their community outreach through SCAs. As a result of this successful partnership, HOPE's network now offers SCAs in partnership with the local church in several countries around the world.

- *Five Talents International (www.fivetalents.org)* pioneered SCAs around the world with leaders of the Anglican Church. Five Talents was founded at the Lambeth Conference in 1998 and was charged with helping the Anglican Church create long-term solutions to poverty throughout the developing world. Five Talents helps families fight poverty, create jobs, and transform lives through microfinance with a particular focus on SCAs.

- *World Relief (www.worldrelief.org)* has worked for over 70 years to "empower the local church to serve the most vulnerable." They do this through a number of initiatives, including disaster response, health and child development, refugee and immigration services, economic development, and peacebuilding. SCAs are one element of their work in economic development.

- *Medical Ambassadors International (www.medicalambassadors. org)* is a Christian organization that offers Community Health Evangelism programs to train communities to invest in holistic development. MAI hosts training seminars in related skills, including establishing SCAs, with the aim of making positive improvements in the living conditions of people in poverty. MAI works to help prevent disease, protect clean water sources, devise sanitation systems, and increase agricultural productivity.

CHALLENGES

SCAs are poised to reach hundreds of thousands of additional families. They are simple, yet effective. They avoid many of the problems associated with external involvement since their very design requires local ownership and participation. They require a fraction of the funding required to start a microfinance institution. They complement the activities of the local church and hold enormous promise for putting entrepreneurs on the pathway out of poverty. But they do not provide quick fixes or overnight successes.

The key question is whether the Church in the U.S. will have the patience to promote and support a type of activity that results in lasting yet incremental change. Or will the Church migrate back to a system of handouts that provides immediate—but temporary—results? Our hope is that an increased focus on SCAs will be one indicator that the Church is "in" for the long term and recognizes that some of the greatest impacts are seen over years, not days.

12

Getting Beyond the Starting Gate

(PHIL)

Southern Hills Country Club is one of the truly great golf courses in the United States. Its elevated first tee overlooks a dogleg fairway and the skyline of downtown Tulsa. On a typical round, if one of the two traps on the right doesn't grab my ball, it's probably because I hit into the oak trees on the left. As I played a recent round with Tom Litteer—and as he stroked a 285-yard drive down the center of the fairway—he asked me, "Would you write one chapter for people like the ones in my church?"

We had been talking about the contents of this book, and Tom wanted to be able to recommend it to his parishioners in New Jersey. As we drove our cart down the hillside, he said, "You see, the people in my church are good-hearted, sincere Christians who want to show the love of Christ. But they are all pretty busy with their jobs and families. Could you write a chapter that just describes, step by step, how we might get involved in microfinance?"

Although that request sounded simple enough, I already knew some of the traps. I told some of my other friends, "Writing my first book was much simpler because religion was not involved. When you write to Christians, it's much more difficult to wade through theology, emotions, and beliefs." However, I believe Jesus would not have commanded us to share the Gospel in both Word and deed unless there were practical ways to do it. So this chapter is for the folks in Tom's church and anyone else who wants to make a difference using microfinance but isn't sure how to get started.

CONSTRAINTS

The first step in choosing the best way to become involved with microfinance is to understand your own constraints, desires, and opportunities. Through experience, I know that after learning about microfinance, many people and churches become enamored enough to want to start their own MFIs. As you consider that possibility, ask yourself several questions:

- *What human resources can I commit?* Operating a microfinance institution is as complicated as running a bank in the United States. That makes it beyond the scope of most churches or individuals. The complexity requires administrative know-how and an understanding of complex regulatory environments. Unless you have a substantial amount of human resources at your disposal, you are not likely to be able to start an MFI of any size.

- *What financial resources can I commit?* I often have people write for advice whose dreams and desires far outdistance their financial resources. Although these are not exact costs, the following may give you an idea of the high cost of providing microfinance: Providing one loan might cost $50 to $1,000; funding a community bank with an existing MFI might cost $5,000 to $25,000; funding for an existing MFI to move into a new country might cost $300,000 to $1 million; funding to start a new MFI might be $500,000 to $5 million.

- *What other resources can I commit?* God has provided us many resources and talents to use. For instance, you may not have any available financial resources, but you might be able to communicate with an MFI on a regular basis. Using this information, you might convince your small group to join you in regular prayer for the efforts of the MFI. Much more will be said about this in a later chapter.

- *What conflicts of interest might arise if my church launches its own MFI?* Whenever I think about a church starting an MFI, I am reminded of something a microfinance professional once told me: "Christians do not always make good borrowers—they believe in grace, not works. If they don't pay back their loans, they expect complete forgiveness." As you start thinking about pastors handling large amounts of cash or trying to collect loans from church members, it's easy to see the potential conflicts.

- *Will running an MFI be a bigger distraction than it's worth?* Again, an MFI is a complex operation. Other than very small projects, microfinance demands full-time, experienced professionals. Unless microfinance is the primary function of your organization, it may very possibly be a distraction, and a failed microfinance endeavor could even endanger the quality of your witness.

INDIA

Now that we have asked the questions to set the foundation, let's consider the basics of getting involved with microfinance using MFIs.

STEP BY STEP

Fortunately, there are many ways for Christians and churches to become involved with MFIs. Keeping the above questions in mind, here are some of the most likely possibilities:

Advocate

To say I bombard my wife and friends with talk of microfinance is an understatement—maybe that's why I don't get invited to many parties. I love to talk about the benefits of microfinance and how it so cost effectively helps people in poverty and can be used to share the Gospel. Over the past year, I met many other passionate advocates of microfinance. These people serve as informal educators and are the reason why many faith-based organizations, civic organizations, nonprofits, and individuals have gotten involved with this life-changing concept. By telling people in your networks about microfinance, you might help others involve their time, energy, money, and prayer in this worthy endeavor.

Make a Donation

A donation of virtually any size can help an existing MFI, especially if there are no strings attached. Although you might be able to earmark your donation for a particular country or project, it is unlikely that you can expect much input into the use of your donation unless it is quite large. One way donors who want to invest a modest amount can get involved is through Kiva at *www.kiva.org*. This organization allows people to make small loans to individuals in other countries through existing MFIs. The amounts needed are relatively small—investments start at $25—so it can be a good way for children or youth groups to contribute. For less than we typically spend on eating out, we can make a practical difference in the life of a brother or sister in poverty. Although Kiva is not a Christian organization, it does partner with Christ-centered field partners like HOPE International and is a way for people to become acquainted with the concept of microfinance.

Fund a Community Bank

Many MFIs would be pleased to have you or your church fund a community bank loan portfolio. All Souls Unitarian Church of Tulsa, Oklahoma, has funded 32 of FINCA International's community banks located in Nicaragua, Guatemala, Mexico, Haiti, the Democratic Republic of Congo, and Kyrgyzstan. The members of All Souls have raised money through bake sales, dinners, youth group service projects, and holiday sales. All Souls not only asks its members to support these banks but endeavors to enlist the support of the wider community in Tulsa.

Involve Your Business

FLYJOY makes delicious snack bars, and they've built a business model that directly incorporates generosity, giving 10 percent of all profits to HOPE International's work. The company also puts information about HOPE on each snack bar wrapper. An entrepreneur himself, founder Curtis Bomgaars resonates with the nonprofit's mission: "HOPE provides the support and freedom each client needs in order to not only grow their business, but to also grow as individuals."

Lend to an MFI

For those interested in investing larger amounts of money, typically $100,000 or more, lending money to MFIs at low interest rates may be an option. These funds are put to work helping people in poverty while, at the same time, making a small profit for the lenders. Loans can be made either directly to institutions or through funds which diversify among many MFIs. As a lender, remember that it's as harmful for MFIs to take on too much debt as it is for clients. Take time to research the MFI to ensure it is not getting in over its head.

Actively Support an Existing Organization

When Mars Hill Bible Church in Grandville, Michigan, considered international engagement, they partnered with Turame Community Finance, a microfinance institution in Burundi. This partnership was regularly featured in Mars Hill's materials, website, and sermons. Willowdale Chapel in Kennett Square, Pennsylvania, took a similar approach when partnering with HOPE in the Democratic Republic of Congo and Burundi.

In these examples, both the implementing organizations and the churches in the United States have learned valuable lessons about what makes a successful partnership. Don Golden, former executive pastor at Mars Hill, described the changing face of partnership this way: "The history of dominance among parachurch agencies calls for a special willingness to relinquish control and to foster a shared mission agenda." Gone are the days of passive partnerships. Instead, both implementers and churches are ready for a "live" relationship, marked by the following:

Limited focus to one geographic area: Both Mars Hill and Willowdale Chapel recognized that by focusing their efforts on a few particular areas, it would be possible to increase the "ownership" their church body feels. You might like having more dots on your "map" of places that you're serving, but focusing on fewer areas allows you to actually know the people you're partnering with. Long-term relationships matter. Arguably, three trips to the same place to develop relationships make a more significant impact than three trips to different places.

Information flow: It is far better to overcommunicate in these partnerships, while respecting the time constraints and technology challenges field offices face. Without regular contact with church members, partnerships grow cold. Regularly scheduled bulletin inserts, pictures on slides, videos, and updates directly from the field are each critical. During a church service at Willowdale, the pastor made a telephone call to the managing director in the Democratic Republic of Congo so his congregation could hear an update.

Visits: Despite advances in communication technology, there is still no substitute for face-to-face interaction. Annual trips by a few key members of a congregation help keep foreign partnerships immediate. Additionally, church members with specific skills can bring insight and training to in-country staff. Jim Krimmel is a professor at Messiah College, a certified public accountant, and a certified fraud examiner. Krimmel traveled to the Philippines, the Democratic Republic of Congo, and Ukraine with HOPE International to lead fraud prevention training and conduct assessments on the internal controls for loan disbursements and repayments.

Engagement by church members: Qualified and interested church members, interns, and staff members are key in developing relationships with an MFI. There are certainly ways to connect individuals who are gifted in finance, marketing, and writing to the organization's short- and long-term needs, as will be discussed later.

CHOOSING A MICROFINANCE ORGANIZATION

To finish our step-by-step instruction in how to become involved in microfinance, here are some suggestions about choosing a particular MFI as a

MALAWI

partner. There are thousands of microfinance organizations, so the following represents a synthesis of what I typically recommend.

The process starts with finding out which constraints mentioned in the first part of this chapter are most important to you. Depending on the answers, other questions will follow. Does the project need to be done in a specific community or country? Is a particular type of project required in addition to microfinance, such as clean water or AIDS education? Must the project be overtly Christ-centered?

If somebody wants to invest in microfinance or if the project must be done in a specific community or country, I recommend using MIX Market, *www.mixmarket.org*. Search MIX Market profiles to view important statistics for over 2,000 MFIs. By reviewing the websites of the various organizations, you can usually narrow your choices down to a few organizations.

In the event you want to deal with a multinational MFI network, some of the ones you might consider are Accion International, FINCA International, Pro Mujer, and HOPE International. There are other multinational aid organizations which also engage in microfinance, including World Concern, World Relief, and World Vision.

The number of microfinance organizations consistently and clearly sharing the Gospel is small. Of these, many are MFIs that work in only one country and can best be found through MIX Market as described above. If you want to support an MFI that overtly proclaims the Gospel, take the time to review their annual reports, websites, and other materials, and then talk to several people who work there. Don't be afraid to ask detailed questions about how they are practically sharing the Gospel to make sure they are truly doing so in a way you desire.

MICROFINANCE AND RELATIONSHIPS

Microfinance is about more than providing financial services. The most powerful aspect of microfinance as it relates to the Great Commission may be its ability to form lasting, deep relationships, typically between the borrower and the MFI's loan officer. These relationships are valuable opportunities for evangelism and life-changing discipleship.

Ji Shan (name changed for security) owns a cosmetic business in East Asia and used small loans to help it grow after her husband left her and their young daughter. As she took out loans, she began to develop a relationship with her loan officer, who provided support as she healed from her divorce. Through this relationship, Ji Shan eventually came to know an eternal hope and is now an active member in her local fellowship, even hosting a weekly study group in her home.

The business environment is where people spend much of their waking time, develop friendships, and gain the respect of their peers. It would have been difficult to initially invite Ji Shan to church, but it was easy for her loan officer to develop a business relationship that modeled and shared Christ's love.

Participating in a microfinance venture can sometimes be daunting, but the rewards are significant. However, it's important to be aware of a number of pitfalls awaiting Christ-centered microfinance efforts, which we'll discuss in the next chapter.

13

Pastors Seldom Make Good Bankers

(PETER)

A pastor in Rwanda told me he had tried to launch a microfinance program several years earlier. With a rueful chuckle, he described how disastrous it was and how he lost two things.

> First, I lost money as people assumed that money coming from the church was a grant, not a loan. Second, I lost people in my church. If individuals were late on payments, they would not come to church. Perhaps they were nervous that I'd ask for their repayment as they were leaving the church, or that I'd preach a difficult message targeted right at them. It just didn't work.

This pastor recognized that it is possible to harm the church while trying to do acts of service. Inappropriately organized or administered microfinance supports the Swahili proverb "*Kiaribucho urafiki ni kukopa na kuazima*"—"that which spoils friendship is borrowing and lending."[1]

From personal experience, I know that if the design of a microfinance project is wrong, there will be virtually no end to the difficulties. Relationships will be strained and ministries will be ineffective. The tools described in this book could have a negative effect if used improperly. It is our hope that we can save you some of the heartache many others have already experienced.

This chapter highlights several important cautions that will help improve the chances of success when implementing microfinance. It is divided into two sections: operational issues and specific challenges for the Church.

OPERATING WITH EXCELLENCE

When creating or managing a microfinance institution, there are internal operational issues that significantly influence the likelihood of running a successful program.

Internal Controls

Nothing hurts the ministry of a church more than moral failure. I have heard of several Westerners who wanted to support local entrepreneurs by giving funds to local churches, expecting the money would be used properly. "We trust the local pastors and entrepreneurs—we know they have good hearts." This is a common sentiment, yet we could actually be placing our brothers and sisters in serious temptation.

It would be beyond foolish to encourage a pastor, while on the road, to share a hotel room with a person of the opposite sex, or for a pastor to take up the offering every Sunday without any oversight. Who would willingly place a leader in these tempting situations? In the same way, simply handing large amounts of money to our brothers and sisters overseas, relying exclusively on trust, is often setting them up to fail, both financially and morally. If we are serious about assisting, we do them a greater service by first installing strong systems of internal controls and accountability.

Although the amounts of money involved in microfinance might seem small compared to U.S. standards, they easily amount to *years* of wages for any one person in Bangladesh or Malawi or Peru. It is not fair to tempt church

DEMOCRATIC REPUBLIC OF CONGO

leaders with these amounts of money when their families and friends may be faced with immediate financial needs. Imagine a local pastor who receives a large sum of money to be used in microfinance on the same day he learns that a member of his congregation is HIV-positive and needs medicine. Local church leaders and pillars within the Christian community have brought shame to the Church's mission—sometimes with good intentions and sometimes maliciously—that could have been prevented with rigorous controls to minimize temptation and ensure that funds were used according to their intended purpose.

Count the Cost

A woman who had served as a lifelong missionary in Africa inherited $10,000. With excitement in her voice, she described how she had heard of microfinance and that she was interested in having our organization begin a new microfinance institution in the community where she had served. I didn't want to dampen her excitement, but the reality was that $10,000 is not sufficient capital to launch a microfinance institution.

This woman is not alone. Starting a full-fledged microfinance institution is an extremely costly venture. You need appropriate systems that can track repayments and loan officer performance. You need enough capital to support an administrative office. You need the expertise to navigate the regulatory requirements of central banks. Doing quality microfinance normally requires funding in the seven-figure range for each country of service—and you can't count past the decimal point!

The Right Skills

Many people and organizations now starting microfinance programs have previously been focused on traditional charity and missions. However, microfinance requires a different skill set. If you haven't balanced your checkbook recently, it's likely you aren't the right person to lead a new business venture.

Sustainability and Interest Rates

One of the most powerful aspects of microfinance is that it can cover its operating costs. This allows an entity to operate over many years or even decades even if external funding stops. Achieving this goal requires an interest rate sufficient to cover local operating costs. There are too many examples of MFIs that have fizzled out due to insufficient revenue, leaving loan recipients little better off than they were before. The entrepreneurs most MFIs serve are looking for financial services they can trust over the life of their business, not another short-term project.

Take Repayments Seriously

Since we're focused on helping people living in poverty, shouldn't we just forgive the few borrowers who might not be able to pay back a loan? Surely we don't need the money as much as they do, right? This common sentiment will not only cause repayment rates to plummet, but it also has the potential to hurt the community in the long term as local individuals will be conditioned not to repay. Once the "credit well" is poisoned, it is difficult for other groups to operate successfully in the area. If entrepreneurs did not repay the last microfinance institution, they assume that the word "credit" is really just a disguised grant. And when grants are mixed with loans, all you get are groans!

Work with the Government

Governments get squeamish when outsiders enter their country to lend money. And for good reason. There are too many examples of unscrupulous behavior in the lending industry around the world for regulators to turn a blind eye. They know that lack of trust in financial institutions sends shock waves throughout an economy. Those lending money and engaging in savings must do so in a way that builds the financial infrastructure of a country. MFIs need to cooperate with laws and requirements of local officials in good faith and to the best of their ability.

KEEPING THE MISSION

While these issues are common to anyone engaged in microfinance, the following challenges are specific to churches engaged in this form of poverty alleviation.

Avoid Rice Christianity

When some of the first English missionaries to Asia confronted the region's grinding poverty some 200 years ago, they saw the people's dire need for rice and gave away all the rice they could. They persuaded churches in England to donate money for rice, which they purchased locally and distributed to those in need. The missionaries were sincere and well-meaning, and as long as they provided rice, members of the community attended church—the size of services increased substantially. But when the rice ran out, the churches emptied. These church folk became known as "rice Christians."

Good works, like offerings of rice or capital, are a critical part of serving Jesus Christ, but when they are used in a way that rewards religious involvement, the resulting faith of the followers is most likely shallow or nonexistent. When an MFI only offers its services to Christians, it can appear to be bribing people into the Kingdom of God. This is not the biblical understanding of service. Unfortunately, even when the Church doesn't intend to do this, others can still misunderstand the Church's motivation. This is one reason why we encourage microfinance institutions to love and serve all with equal treatment and not to show partiality when evaluating potential clients.

Keep the Mission Central

Healthy organizations grow and develop. Unwillingness to adapt to changing circumstances is a recipe for stagnancy and irrelevance. Yet an organization can adapt so much that there is nothing left of the original. Many organizations founded on Christ have drifted away from their original mission to the extent that their founding principles are no longer recognizable.

Consider Barclay's Bank. Its original mission statement was "to create honorable employment and beneficial businesses that honor God." Founding documents describe how each day was to begin with prayer, and faith was to be infused into every aspect of the bank's operations.[2] Looking at Barclay's today, it is difficult to find evidence of these religious roots or founding practices.

After hearing a presentation on HOPE International, several executives from a leading nonprofit organization that builds homes expressed their surprise at how overt we are about our faith and asked, "Aren't you worried that you will offend some people?" I later learned that less than 15 years ago, their organization was open about faith. But this candle was snuffed out after they discovered individuals outside the organization did not approve of the "religious" elements of their work. To accommodate a wider audience—and secure more funding—they slowly walked away from their original motivation and methodology.

Guarding against gradual mission drift requires an intentional approach that connects the actions and practices of an organization to its mission. At HOPE International, ensuring that we have an impact on physical and spiritual poverty is at the core of our identity. We believe this combination of sharing the Gospel and providing financial services is key to lasting transformation for families in poverty. To protect this spiritual focus, we prioritize Christ-centeredness first in our strategic planning, focus on discipling our staff, routinely monitor our progress on key spiritual metrics, and hire people with not

PHILIPPINES

only the right skills but the right hearts for ministry—people with the head of a banker but the heart of a pastor.

Partner with the Local Church

The former Anglican archbishop of Rwanda, Emmanuel Kolini, described an experience he had with a prominent Christian relief and development organization engaged in microfinance. "When they arrived in Rwanda, they asked us for our help. We helped them register, find the right connections, and set up their operations. Yet as soon as things were moving, they turned their back on the local church."

Ignoring the local church is not an option for organizations devoted to Christ. Not only will the local church outlast foreign organizations, but the local church is often the most influential institution in a community. It would be a waste not to use the most obvious and beneficial resource available. Further, for long-term benefits for the Kingdom, it is imperative to grow local church leadership and improve the lives of members. They are God's hands and feet in those communities, and we are stronger when we work closely with them as part of the same body.

The HOPE International director in one Asian country had a passion for unreached people and was pushing the frontier on microfinance. A survey of all loan recipients in one branch discovered that more than half of the clients said they heard about Jesus Christ for the very first time through HOPE. Individuals were seeing the benefit of microfinance and hearing about the love of Jesus Christ—and they were responding.

Unfortunately, the local church was simply nonexistent, and these individuals were left without access to further spiritual development. In an area where freedom of religion is severely restricted by the government, there were few options. HOPE did not have the ability or expertise to launch churches or disciple clients to become fully devoted followers of Christ. HOPE had helped spread the Gospel and introduced many to Jesus Christ but was unable to see these new Christians grow in maturity.

Young Christians need spiritual guidance, so we now focus on working in areas that have a local church presence or partner with a church-planting ministry. This allows us to ensure that newly believing clients can become part of healthy churches.

Measure and Compare Results

A survey tracked funding released by the Ministry of Finance in Chad that was intended for rural health clinics. The survey's goal was to determine how much of the funding actually reached the clinics. It was not concerned with whether the clinics spent it well or even if it made a positive impact on the community, only with whether it arrived. The findings were shocking. Research concluded that "less than 1 percent of [the funding] reached the clinics—99 percent failed to reach its destination."[3] Where was the accountability?

Accountability is a bedrock principle in the business world, where the clear bottom line of profit makes it possible to assess performance. However, nonprofit organizations often have little accountability and few techniques with which to allocate more resources to the most effective programs. Nonprofits—and for-profit MFIs—must decide what to monitor and how to monitor it in order to ensure performance.

Measuring performance indicators like the total amount of money loaned, repayment rates, and return on equity are necessary to build a high-performing MFI. Measuring impact in the realm of Christ-centered microfinance is much more difficult. Along with providing loans, how do we know if individuals are growing in their faith or even becoming less hostile to the claims of Jesus? Unfortunately, too often "the quality of fundraising literature ... seems to matter far more than the quality of work."[4] There is virtually no oversight of what organizations do: "They are continents away from the people who've entrusted them with their cash."[5]

Despite the difficulty, there needs to be accountability—we *all* need it! For example, in addition to external audits and agency ratings, HOPE International has a spiritual integration team to help assess the spiritual impact of our efforts. This team coordinates with local leadership to ensure that each country is monitoring and measuring culturally appropriate activities and results. This tracking includes everything from the number of church partners to the impact on clients participating in discipleship groups. We believe this monitoring will help guide holistic impact on the lives of clients.

Given the significant challenges inherent in operating a successful microfinance institution, many organizations see partnerships as an attractive option. Specifically, churches that partner with microfinance institutions become voices that are critical in protecting the organization's mission. In the next chapter, we'll discuss practical ways your church or small group can get involved.

ZIMBABWE

14

Rolling Up Our Sleeves

(PHIL)

How many times did you think about poverty last week? The prophet Amos had harsh words for Israel, calling them "cows of Bashan" (Amos 4:1) for neglecting those in poverty. Amos outlines God's distaste for the way they "oppress the poor and crush the needy" (v. 1) and warns, "Though you have built stone mansions, you will not live in them; though you have planted lush vineyards, you will not drink their wine" (Amos 5:11). Forgetting people in poverty is unthinkable to God.

Yet for us, forgetting is all too easy. We do not see the men in poverty in Zambia when we leave our suburban homes and drive to work. We do not see the children in poverty in Cambodia during our lunch breaks. We might see the women in poverty in Peru only on television—but it's easy to change the channel.

This is why we need reminders. This is why the pages of our Bibles—from Genesis to the prophets of the Israelites, and from Jesus to Paul—consistently command us to "remember the poor." Turning a blind eye is sinful, but it is quick and painless, particularly since we live in a culture where we're bombarded by countless advertisements every day showing us what *we* don't have. They shout the lie that we'd be more popular, sexy, and satisfied if only we had a better outfit, cell phone, flat screen TV, or car. What we really need are constant reminders of what we *do* have and how we can act to impact those who have far less. Maybe then we will roll up our sleeves and actually do something about it.

ON YOUR KNEES, PLEASE

How often do we say "I'll pray for you"—and how often do we really pray? In Scripture, prayer is often like a wrestling match. As pastor and author Rick Warren writes:

> People may refuse our love or reject our message, but they are defenseless against our prayers. ... The Bible tells us to pray for opportunities to witness, for courage to speak up, for those who will believe, for the rapid spread of the message, and for more workers. ... You should also pray for missionaries and everyone else involved in the global harvest. Paul told his prayer partners, "You are also joining to help us when you pray for us" (2 Corinthians 1:11).[1]

INDIA

Prayer focuses us on what is important. Praying for those in poverty can open our eyes to their reality and connect our hearts with theirs. In an amazing way, prayer has the potential to change us even as we are praying for others. James writes, "The prayer of a righteous person is powerful and effective" (James 5:16). Our prayers are heard by a loving God who loves to respond. Consider joining the prayer update list of missions-minded microenterprise development organizations and remembering staff, employees, and clients in regular prayer.

LESS IS MORE

Tony Campolo is considered by some to be a modern-day William Wilberforce with regard to social justice issues. He is a living reminder not to forget those on the margins. Unconventional in his approach, Campolo is focused on pricking the evangelical conscience in order to prompt action. In *Everybody Wants to Change the World*, Campolo and Gordon Aeschliman describe one movement designed to help us remember people in poverty.

One simple idea for combating compassion fatigue is to try to live once a month on less than $2 a day, like 949 million people do every day. Commit to doing this for a year with a group of friends who also want to go on the same spiritual journey of keeping families in poverty alive in their hearts. After the year is up, evaluate how the discipline has shaped your lifestyle and commitments regarding the needs of others. Living on less than $2 will be a challenge because you will have to deprive your body for 24 hours. You will have to fast for the day—or eat a can of soup that you purchased for less than $2. Your beverage will consist of glasses of water from the faucet. And you won't be able to drive far, because you'd use up $2 of fuel in a short distance.

Christmas may be the best time of the year to engage children in remembering the example and life of Jesus instead of celebrating consumerism gone crazy. Followers of Jesus could use this time of year to focus on the joys that come from giving to others, restoring a degree of sanity to the holiday. Jenn Knepper of Pennsylvania celebrates Christmas with her nieces and nephews by pulling together a portion of their allowances that they have saved throughout the year and looking through the materials of Heifer International, World Vision, and Samaritan's Purse to pick out gifts to give to others around the world. In 2008, Jenn brought this idea to a wider group of people through the Gifts that Give Hope fair in Lancaster, Pennsylvania. Like other alternative gift fairs, it offers people giving opportunities with service-focused organizations. Instead of shopping mania on Black Friday, shoppers can purchase gift cards supporting local and international charities. All of these types of efforts are attempting to combat the perception of many Americans who "honestly think we have barely enough to survive in modest comfort."[2]

VOLUNTEERING

Another way to remember people in developing countries is through volunteering. PEER Servants is an organization connecting volunteers directly to microfinance institutions around the world. By breaking individuals into teams that maximize the skills and abilities of each member, they have proven meaningful engagement is possible, even from a distance.

Take the example of Ron Olofernes, who serves as relationship manager with PEER Servants' partner in the Philippines, the Center for Community Transformation. Originally from the Philippines himself, Ron shares, "As a volunteer with PEER Servants, I've found a meaningful opportunity to use my God-given skills and abilities while providing a positive impact in the lives of the materially poor, especially in my home country. Since the start of my volunteering work with PEER Servants, I have felt that my heart towards helping the materially poor has grown."[3]

PEER Servants is a leader in connecting volunteers to ministry opportunities, but many other organizations provide opportunities as well, and several do so through relationships with the Halftime movement. Bob Buford's book *Halftime* inspired thousands of individuals in the second half of their lives to seek service opportunities. Many of these individuals have business skills critical to building employment-based solutions to poverty. Since microenterprise development is essentially banking for individuals in poverty, it is a natural place for bankers and the business community to devote their skills to a very different group of shareholders. The same skills that led to success in the first half of life can be applied in amazing ways in the second half.

David Foster is one such individual. A certified public accountant, David spent 24 years working for such organizations as Ernst & Young and CENIT Bank, where he created the internal controls department and served as vice president and director of operations analysis and internal controls. Since officially retiring in 2014, David has traveled with HOPE International to Malawi and Rwanda, where he volunteers his extensive experience to help with operational and financial audits. "Given my prior experience in banking, auditing, and volunteering," David shares, "it seemed like a perfect fit for me to volunteer my services to an organization such as HOPE. Like most volunteer activities, I receive much more from the experience than I could have ever imagined."

PERU

LEARN TOGETHER

Your small group or church can easily learn more about a biblical understanding of poverty, its causes, and its remedies. Some of what you and your fellow Christ-followers find may spur you into action. Here are a few helpful resources:

- *Hope Lives* is a curriculum written by Compassion International staff member Amber Van Schooneveld. This five-week study also has a children's version so you can study issues of global poverty with your whole family.

- In partnership with Willowdale Chapel, HOPE International produced *Perspectives on Global Poverty*, an eight-week Bible study that examines God's heart for families in poverty and challenges believers to take concrete action in response. *perspectives.hopeinternational.org*

SEE IT TO BELIEVE IT

Sometimes you need to see something to understand it. Greg Thompson, an entrepreneur from Massachusetts, described the impact of seeing microfinance firsthand: "I had heard about microfinance but was blown away when I actually saw it. It was like watching fireworks on television versus actually being underneath the explosions ... like watching a movie about a roller coaster versus being in the front seat of one. It's just so much more incredible in person."[4]

These experiences can prompt individuals to take significant action. Justin Bredeman was an executive with Auntie Anne's pretzel-franchising company prior to traveling to the Dominican Republic to learn about microenterprise development along with me and several others. He explained, "Meeting individuals who were working themselves out of poverty, hearing their stories firsthand, visiting their homes, and meeting their children had a much bigger impact on me than I ever expected. There is a way of helping people help themselves, and I wanted to be a part of it."

But what should you do when you return from a short-term mission trip? Is it enough to return from a trip and feel more thankful for all that you have? That's a start. But if that is the only fruit after a direct encounter with poverty, something is missing. Seeing such needs with our own eyes creates a responsibility to actually *do* something.

Unfortunately, the statistics are not encouraging about the way short-term trips move people to action. Kurt Ver Beek, director of Calvin College's Honduras Program, has dedicated a significant part of his research to the effec-

RWANDA

tiveness of short-term missions. In an interview, *Christianity Today* magazine reported on his findings:

> While 52 percent of respondents claimed to have increased their giving to the sending organization after the trip, according to the organization's records 70 percent of the participants in their STM [short-term mission] trips to Honduras didn't send in a single direct donation in the three years after the trip ... [and] few lasting friendships were built. While 92 percent of the North Americans said they had meaningful contact with Hondurans for at least part of every day of their trip, less than a quarter stayed in touch with their Honduran friends after they returned home.[5]

Although the results found by Ver Beek may not reflect the impact of every short-term mission trip, there is no doubt that short-term missions have exploded in popularity. There ought to be a way to discover which people were truly impacted by their experience and engage them quickly after the trip. We are missing a big opportunity if the Church does not find better ways to translate these positive experiences into long-term action.

GIVING WITH EXCELLENCE

The primary way most of us engage those in developing countries is through giving. Two thousand years ago, the apostle Paul told the church members at Corinth that they already excelled "in everything—in faith, in speech, in knowledge, in complete earnestness and in the love we have kindled in you" (2 Corinthians 8:7). Then he went on to exhort them to "see that you also excel in this grace of giving." How can we 21st-century Christians excel at the grace of giving?

Don Millican is the CFO of a successful company, a former partner of a "Big Four" accounting firm, and a long-time church leader. He asks some clarifying questions about excellent giving. Does it mean to give effectively?

If so, how do we define effectiveness and gather the data to measure it? Does it mean to give according to what we feel are the leadings of the Holy Spirit? If so, how do we quantify those leadings and implement them in our lives? How do we even understand how we fit in the process of giving?

Millican points to 1 Corinthians 3:6-7 as an important passage showing that God is responsible for the results of our giving, not us. "I planted the seed, Apollos watered it, but God has been making it grow. So neither the one who plants nor the one who waters is anything, but only God, who makes things grow." From our earthly point of view we cannot see how effective some programs have been, are, or may be in the future. Millican asks, "What if you only impact one person for Christ, and that person turns out to be the next Billy Graham?"

He also says we are to be good stewards of the resources entrusted to us, and, in that capacity, we have to make the best giving decisions we can, given the information we have. Being an excellent giver often means living at the intersection of faith and action.

Our giving resources consist of time, talent, and treasure. If we think about it this way, we realize that our time and talent are mostly constrained by our physical location. For that reason, our time and talent are often best allocated to our local communities. Our treasure is our "stored labor." We can easily ship our stored labor anywhere in the world at any time. So, if efficiency is the point, our treasure is often the resource best used in developing countries.

Our treasure doesn't consist only of the money in our bank accounts. We have many unexpected sources of treasure available if we just look around for them. The high school leadership group at First United Methodist Church in Birmingham, Michigan, met one afternoon in 2005. They decided to implement a new project to reach their own community about the problem of HIV and AIDS in Africa. Their plan was to collect 23 million pennies representing the 23 million people infected with HIV and AIDS in sub-Saharan Africa—and they did! These funds were used to sponsor several African health and educational organizations.

After a lot of Scripture study, Millican and I have come to understand that the Bible seems to address three categories of giving. As we allocate resources between and within these three categories, we must rely on prayer; the wise counsel of church leaders and other Christians; and the Holy Spirit's still, small voice.

- **Church:** We're called to support our local churches financially. We entrust these funds to the congregation's leaders, who have been chosen by God. As members of the community, we are called to rely on the group's leadership and support its prayerful actions. This type of giving makes up the majority of giving for many U.S. Christians, and it also made up the majority of giving for Jews and Christians in the early days of the Church. Leadership—not the givers—is primarily responsible for how effectively these gifts are spent.

- **Compassion:** We are called to give compassionately to meet the immediate needs of people in our lives, especially our families and other Christians. Although Christ calls us to give generously and even sacrificially, we must be careful not to create dependency. In this type of giving, we are to rely on the Holy Spirit to help us discern how we respond. Our end goal is to see that needs are met and that God receives the glory.

- **Calling:** We are individually called to spread the Kingdom by helping people, both physically and spiritually. Those of us who are rich—and that's *all* of us!—have the ability to make a significant and lasting impact in developing countries.

But how specifically should we allocate our resources to make a difference for Jesus Christ? How do we put biblical principles and commandments into action? The way we allocate our resources is where we roll up our sleeves and put our money where our mouths are.

I'd like to offer some ideas based on my own giving and the experiences of people and churches I have worked with over the years. The most common tendency of givers (and missions committees) is to give money away this year very much like it was given the previous year. Sometimes this happens after intensive analysis, but more often it happens for a variety of other reasons such as habit, the desire not to hurt somebody's feelings, or responding to pleas from friends.

Our actions could be entirely different if we chose to follow clear guidelines. For instance, in the past I have chosen to allocate money based on the effectiveness of individual projects, but now I try to allocate based on a project's ability to help people both spiritually and physically on a long-term basis. Because I have changed my guidelines, the results of how I give have changed dramatically.

As an example, consider an evangelist who might propose going to India and presenting the gospel to 10,000 people over two weeks at a cost of

DEMOCRATIC REPUBLIC OF CONGO

$20,000. He believes he will be able to preach to that number of people but has not coordinated the effort with local Christians for follow-up relationship building. In the past I would have found this to be a good project because sharing the Gospel at $2 per person seems very efficient. Today I would not support the project because by definition it would not meet people's physical and spiritual needs over the long term.

Let me point out that every giver will spend his or her giving budget using some method and some set of assumptions. The fact that the money gets spent shows that value judgments and allocation techniques have been made and used, whether explicitly or implicitly. Since every giving expenditure is evaluated in *some* way, doesn't it make sense to evaluate our choices thoughtfully and intentionally? Some people believe their allocations and judgments are made solely through the leading of the Holy Spirit, but taking the time to pray and think through our giving decisions is simply a way of fulfilling the steward responsibility God has given us.

HAITI

Here's some good news that we hope this book has made clear: Microenterprise development and other employment-based poverty alleviation solutions are helping those living in poverty. Giving to these types of projects and to the right organizations is a highly effective way to improve the physical and spiritual condition of people in poverty around the world. We don't need to be afraid of giving. Rather, as we see brave Christ-followers doing holistic work in every country around the world, our only fear may be that we aren't yet giving enough.

CHOOSING ORGANIZATIONS

I believe givers should ask themselves two basic questions when they start assessing whether to support an organization. First, are my goals and the goals of the organization in harmony? Second, does the organization actually try to achieve its stated goals in a way that makes sense to me?

The first question became apparent to me after giving a speech about microfinance. When it was over, a woman chided me, saying, "All you care about is poor people. I care most about eliminating abuse to pets." Obviously, she and I should support different organizations.

The second question became important to me after I started asking people why the organizations they worked with or supported, some of which were churches, should be considered "Christian." Here are the types of answers I typically received: "Because we feed those in poverty, and Jesus said we should do that"; "Because we provide fresh water for people, which makes their lives better"; "Because some of our field personnel share the Gospel when they think the time is right"; "Because the founders of our organizations were Baptists"; and, "Because some of our board members go to church regularly." These types of answers remind me of one of the first stories Peter ever shared with me.

As part of a training on microenterprise development sponsored by the United States Agency for International Development in Uganda in 1999, Peter had an opportunity to visit a leading MFI. The MFI was well known as a Christian nonprofit organization and was funded in large part by believers in the U.S. Peter found that it used the same methodology and same loan products as a secular MFI working in the area. The more he compared the two organizations, the more he struggled to find any meaningful difference in their services or relationships with borrowers. Neither one demonstrated biblical discipleship or extraordinary care for employees' or clients' physical, emotional, or spiritual needs. What difference did it make that they were called a Christian organization? Was it anything more than a fundraising tool targeting unsuspecting Christian supporters? Unfortunately, there are many so-called faith-based organizations that would be equally hard-pressed to differentiate themselves from secular programs.

Brian Fikkert, founder and president of the Chalmers Center, once told me, "Christian development work must include a clear presentation of the Gospel. Failure to do so denies individuals access to the only real solution to the fundamental causes of poverty." It might sound like an obvious starting point, but unless an organization takes significant care to create a corporate culture that emphasizes effective witness for Christ, they will not share the Gospel consistently. Granted, individuals in any organization have an opportunity to act as witnesses for Jesus. However, sharing the Gospel consistently and at larger scale can only happen when the organization's management makes it a priority.

All of the above is not meant to criticize secular organizations. In fact, as I discuss below, I think it is a wonderful idea to access these organizations for their services or expertise and even to partner with them in the right circumstances. However, since we all have limited resources, we givers should be careful to use our resources to support those organizations that consistently act in accordance with our own calling and purpose.

There are other organizational characteristics to consider as we decide where to direct our time, energy, and money.

Local Church

Sammy Mah, former president of World Relief, regularly talks about the importance of focusing on "the Big K," the "Kingdom of God." Organizations often spend far too much time building their own little kingdoms and missing the bigger picture. We could accomplish so much more if no one cared who gets the credit.

Within this partnership, the indigenous local church must be central. In a small group setting in conjunction with the Peace Plan launch, Rick Warren spoke about the "NGO-ization" of ministry that has replaced the role of the local church. He is largely right. The local church has not been intimately involved in many Christian development projects around the world, much to the detriment of the local church—and to the detriment of the projects. Working with the local church is not easy, yet this Church is, and always will be, Christ's body on earth to whom He entrusts the task of feeding the hungry and clothing the naked.

No organization is better placed for providing and administering social services than the local church. As we've discussed, the local church has the mandate, the credibility, and the connections that yield the most efficient results. By working with a local church, outsiders can take advantage of local resources without appearing to be the solution to every problem. This allows solutions to be locally owned and empowers local churches. The result is longer-term growth and stability.

Helping a local church provide social services also helps it gain the opportunity to share the Gospel with people who might not otherwise hear the Good News. This allows the local church to develop an integrated ministry of meeting people's financial and spiritual needs.

A common hindrance to working with the local church is a lack of reliable local leadership. Sometimes the solution, rather than turning away, is to raise up and train local leaders. This training might involve discipleship, theological education, lifestyle modeling, and meeting whatever other specific needs exist. Unfortunately, this takes years of effort, so other projects may need to be delayed until this can be accomplished. If a project needs to bypass local Christian leaders, it is a danger sign. When Western organizations find themselves in combat with local leaders, it may be a sign that the Western organization is on shaky ground since local people often understand the situation best. On the other hand, it may also be a sign that local leadership is only protecting its turf and needs to be worked with carefully.

Works Well with Others

All programs and churches have limited resources. Whenever it doesn't compromise the mission of the program or church, we should consider leveraging the assets of other organizations. In a small village in the Dominican Republic, I walked by a nicer-than-normal home with a smiling young woman standing in the doorway. An hour later I walked by again, and she was still standing there and smiling. When I asked my host about her situation, I was told the aid organization that employed this young health worker had mostly solved a particular health care situation in that area. They kept her employed even though she had little work to do. As a result, she now spent most of her day standing in the doorway even though neighboring communities desperately needed her expertise. What was needed was a partnership

MOLDOVA

between this local aid organization and neighboring ones in order to best provide for the needs of the greatest number of people.

In the Dominican Republic, Esperanza International was astute enough to observe that many charities and governmental agencies provide numerous services throughout the island, many of which go unused because few people outside of the local community know about them. Esperanza staff now shares with clients any information regarding services that would be beneficial to them. At virtually no cost to Esperanza, its clients are learning about a plethora of additional services.

Partnering with secular agencies is an important issue. As long as the Christian organization is transparent about its core goals and beliefs, there are many bridge-building opportunities. As more and more Christian organizations gain reputations for operational excellence, an increasing number of development professionals will seek them out for collaboration.

Measure Results

Management guru Peter Drucker said, "You get what you measure."[6] If an organization's goal is to see lasting spiritual fruit, then it is important to find indicators that help steer toward more effective programming. Measuring spiritual indicators needs to be done carefully and comprehensively, just as you measure financial indicators.

It is frustrating that many nonprofit organizations aren't interested in knowing their effectiveness, either financially or spiritually. The ones who do publish numbers often measure things that are not terribly important. If you choose to support an organization, make sure you understand what kind of results you can expect to see reported and how those results are measured.

The primary reason to calculate cost efficiency is to wisely steward the resources God provides to accomplish His will as best as we understand it. Without establishing standards and measuring results, there is no standard by which to allocate resources to various programs. This is especially important for churches, since the programs they become involved with require long-term commitments. Without proper communication about expectations, it is likely that problems will result.

However, determining and monitoring the correct measures is often exceptionally difficult, especially when it comes to spiritual impact. When considering financial results, there are many organizations that attempt to measure and compare the effectiveness of various charities and nonprofit organizations. For the microfinance industry, MIX Market is one of the best. It's a web-based information platform linking MFIs worldwide with investors and donors in order to promote greater investment and information flow. With a platform for fair and standardized reporting, organizations and individuals around the world have a convenient way to share information with donors and like-minded organizations. In turn, investors and donors can more easily compare MFIs to decide where money will best be used to serve families in poverty. MIX Market provides data on over 2,000 MFIs, as well as networks, funders, and service providers.

THE KEY ROLE OF DONORS

History reminds us that the Church's involvement in missions and acts of compassion swings like a pendulum. When acts of compassion replace the presentation of the Gospel story, the next tendency is to swing to the other extreme and ignore the scriptural commands to serve and love through deeds. The greatest threat to the Church's full embrace of this new entrepreneurial approach to integrated Word-and-deed missions is the temptation to slowly compromise the incorporation of the Gospel message. Donors have a key role in protecting this aspect of an organization's mission and preventing this drift from occurring.

Celebrating with Goats

(PETER)

After a 24-hour journey from Washington, DC, to Lubumbashi, Democratic Republic of Congo, missions committee members from Willowdale Chapel and I strapped on the seatbelts of a Toyota Land Cruiser for a brain-rattling journey to a small village named Lubanda. Lubanda is located near Congolese mines that are infamous for extracting diamonds and coltanite—a mineral used in cell phones and PlayStations.

We were visiting this village because of a man affectionately called Monsieur L'Abbey. In this small village that didn't have indoor plumbing or electricity, Monsieur L'Abbey radiated contagious joy with his exuberant smile. The spring in his step made him seem taller than his five-foot-five stature. When he welcomed our team at his small brick church, he stated, "Today is a very special day for Lubanda. Thank you for coming."

With grand fanfare in front of the village chief and hundreds of children, Monsieur L'Abbey said their village wanted to provide us with a gift. Four village elders appeared from the side of the building carrying two grown goats, feet tied and bleating uncontrollably. The elders handed me one of the goats, and I held it awkwardly, trying to show my gratefulness for this special gift and masking my uneasiness in holding a squirming goat.

In Lubanda, goats cost around $50. There was no doubt that this was sacrificial giving. Village members were obviously among the 77 percent of Congolese who live on less than $1.90 per day. As if this gift were not enough, we entered Monsieur L'Abbey's home where our hands were washed in a small bucket as an elderly woman poured water from a plastic cup. This cup became her drinking cup moments later. We ate *fufu*—the cassava-based staple—rice, and chicken, and we drank pineapple soda. Why such a warm welcome? Why such sacrificial giving? And why such joy?

Monsieur L'Abbey knew that our visit to Lubanda marked the beginning of a new partnership. HOPE International was beginning to provide small loans and biblically based education to entrepreneurs in the village. He knew that these loans and training had the potential to radically change lives and alleviate severe poverty. He knew that these services would be a tangible demonstration and verbal proclamation of a God who sees and responds to men and women in poverty.

As we walked around his village, I pressed him for why he believed these loans were going to have such a positive impact on his village. I questioned why he was so grateful that we were beginning operations in Lubanda.

His response was simple: "I know this will help our people."

The more we spoke, the more I saw joy in his life—that mysterious joy that defies circumstance. Joy in giving. Joy in serving. Joy in believing that tomorrow has the potential to be better than today. Joy that flowed from a relationship with his Creator. Joy in a place that you might not expect to find it. His joy overflowed to his community and to our small group of invited guests.

Receiving a goat and eating *fufu* with our hands was unforgettable. But the greatest gift Monsieur L'Abbey lavishly gave us was his example of how joy, dignity, and deep satisfaction can be found and shared—in every setting.

This evidence of joy is just one more example of why we passionately believe that SCAs, MFIs, and other employment-based solutions are working. They work because they unlock the potential of families in poverty. They work because they empower entrepreneurs to make a difference in their communities. They work because a hand up is better than a handout. They work because they foster lasting relationships that address physical and spiritual poverty. They work because they produce joy and dignity, antidotes to dependency and despair.

Given these tools, the last remaining question is whether we—the Church and Christians in the West—are going to use them. We are optimistic that this generation will move beyond complacency and good intentions to thoughtful action that will have lasting results. And we hope that in so doing, the Church will be marked by humility and gratitude as we take part in the global mission of seeing families flourish.

RWANDA

Acknowledgments

We never really paid much attention to a book's acknowledgments until writing this book. It always seemed like a list of names that we'd rarely recognize. After going through the writing process, we now know how important those names are! Truly, this book was written with the support and encouragement of so many friends, just a few of whom receive special mention here.

The first edition of this book would not have happened without the photographic brilliance of Jeremy Cowart, the support of Angela Scheff and the Zondervan team, the vision of Greg Daniel, and the collaboration of Rob Bell.

Josh Kwan, Kevin Panicker, and Mark Russell provided special help in organizing our thoughts and challenging our assumptions. Eric Thurman has been a mentor and example to both of us. Without his willingness to introduce us many years ago, this book would not have happened. Paul and Cindy Marty, Andre Barkov, Carlos Pimentel Sanchez, and Ruth Callanta have given us special inspiration as they continually find innovative ways to offer microfinance services and live in ways that point people toward Jesus.

The millions of other entrepreneurs who are bringing transformation to your communities, you inspire and motivate us to do more.

PETER

Special thanks goes to all my friends and team members at HOPE International, past and present. Jeff Rutt and the entire board, thank you for your enthusiastic support of this project and for giving me the privilege of serving with HOPE.

This revised version would not have happened without Erin Longenecker. Her substantial edits and improvements to this version made it a much better book. Dave Wasik, Dan Williams, Kevin Tordoff, Rebecca Svendsen, Isaac Barnes, Sarah Ann Schultz, and Sarah Moon provided additional feedback and revisions. Kristine Frey and Chris Horst once again added their voices. Jeff Brown served as art director, and Grace Engard and Kelly Ryan redesigned the cover and layout. The global HOPE team contributed their photographs, which visually capture the dignity of the families we serve. It is a gift to work with the terrifically talented HOPE team, who uses their many gifts to equip all people to flourish.

Dave Larson, your fingerprints are all over this. Thanks for all you taught me about microfinance and keeping the Gospel central. David Weekley, Rusty Walter, Terry Looper, Wil VanLoh, Tiger Dawson, and John Montgomery—your support, mentoring, and Dominican Republic trips are legendary. Thank you!

Mom and Dad, thanks for living out what it means to authentically follow Jesus. To the rest of my family—I still can't believe you were willing to read a draft while on vacation. Thank you!

Laurel, Keith, Liliana, and Myles—you are the joys and loves of my life. Thank you for being so encouraging of this project and making home a place I always can't wait to get to. Love you!

PHIL

Special thanks to Shannon for giving up hundreds of hours we could have shared together, and to Laura and Mom for editing my scribbles over the last two years.

There are simply too many people to mention who have endured my trial balloons, but Mariann McKinney, Bill Dozier, J. D. Payne, Dave McCabe, Ken Albright, Larry Christian, Larry Akers, and Don Millican deserve special crowns. My special spiritual mentors John Barnett, Mitch Wilburn, Mark Moore, Dave Jewitt, and Bruce Ewing have been patient beyond belief.

Soli Deo Gloria.
Peter Greer
Phil Smith

ZIMBABWE

Notes

FOREWORD

1. Kris Mauren (executive producer), et al., *Poverty, Inc.*, 2015.

INTRODUCTION: GLIMPSES OF POVERTY

1. Throughout this book, we capitalize "Church" when referring to the global Body of Christ and use lower case "church" when referring to its local expression.

2. Since my time in Rwanda, Urwego has gone through a number of name changes, so we use Urwego throughout this book to avoid confusion.

3. "Poverty Overview," *The World Bank*, April 13, 2016, www.worldbank.org/en/topic/poverty/overview.

CHAPTER 1: FLOWER PETALS IN THE FACE

1. Name changed for security.

2. USCIRF, *2016 Annual Report* (Washington, DC: U.S. Commission on International Religious Freedom, 2016), 161, www.uscirf.gov/sites/default/files/USCIRF%202016%20Annual%20Report.pdf.

3. FAO, IFAD, and WFP, *The State of Food Insecurity in the World 2015. Meeting the 2015 international hunger targets: taking stock of uneven progress* (Rome, Italy: FAO, 2015), 8, www.fao.org/3/a4ef2d16-70a7-460a-a9ac-2a65a533269a/i4646e.pdf.

4. Emily Garin, et al., *Committing to Child Survival: A Promise Renewed* (New York, NY: UNICEF, 2015), 10, www.unicef.org/publications/files/APR_2015_9_Sep_15.pdf.

5. "The Millennium Development Goal (MDG 7) drinking water target has been met, but marked disparities persist," *UNICEF Data*, July 2015, www.data.unicef.org/water-sanitation/water.html.

6. "Diarrhoea remains a leading killer of young children, despite the availability of a simple treatment solution," *UNICEF Data*, June 2016, www.data.unicef.org/child-health/diarrhoeal-disease.html.

7. "Literacy among youth is rising, but young women lag behind," *UNICEF Data*, June 2016, www.data.unicef.org/education/literacy.html.

8. UN, "Goal 3: Ensure healthy lives and promote well-being for all at all ages," *Sustainable Development Goals*, accessed August 18, 2016, www.un.org/sustainabledevelopment/health.

9. "Children: reducing mortality," *World Health Organization*, January 2016, www.who.int/mediacentre/factsheets/fs178/en.

10. "Swaziland," *The World Factbook* (Washington, DC: Central Intelligence Agency, 2016), www.cia.gov/library/publications/the-world-factbook/geos/wz.html.

11. Kirk Magelby, "MicroFranchises as a Solution to Global Poverty," November 2005, cybermissions.org/icafe/theory/Microfranchising%20by%20Magleby,%20Nov.%2005.pdf.

12. "Zimbabwe," *The World Factbook* (Washington, DC: Central Intelligence Agency, 2016), www.cia.gov/library/publications/the-world-factbook/geos/zi.html.

13. Asli Demirguc-Kunt, Leora Klapper, Dorothe Singer, and Peter Van Oudheusden. *The Global Findex Database 2014: Measuring Financial Inclusion around the World*, Policy Research Working Paper 7255 (Washington, DC: World Bank, 2015), datatopics.worldbank.org/financialinclusion.

14. "Poverty Overview," *The World Bank*, April 13, 2016, www.worldbank.org/en/topic/poverty/overview.

15. Even though by global standards there are few people living in poverty in the United States, there are real needs all around us. The poverty that exists in the U.S. still causes pain and hopelessness. The Church must be engaged in bringing hope and healing to the physical, emotional, and spiritual needs in our own backyards and neighboring cities. In no way do we desire to dissuade engagement and service or overlook our neighbors in the U.S., for there is still so much more to do. Rather, our desire is to argue for a "both/and" approach that sees needs in the U.S. but does not overlook the needs in other forgotten parts of the world.

16. "The Mountain Man and the Surgeon," *The Economist*, December 20, 2005, www.economist.com/node/5323888.

17. Rakesh Kochhar, "A Global Middle Class Is More Promise than Reality," *Pew Research Center*, August 13, 2015, www.pewglobal.org/2015/07/08/a-global-middle-class-is-more-promise-than-reality.

18. One more disclaimer: It is exceedingly dangerous to write about "the developing world" or "people in poverty," for in each of these categories are individuals who are anything but homogeneous. Only reluctantly do we use these gross generalizations in this book to highlight overall trends. We must never forget that individuals living in poverty are individuals; there are no "average" people. Each person has a name, a mother, a father, and their own story. Each has emotions, dreams, and desires. God made each one with the same care He used in making each and every one of us. It is appropriate that we should consider every one of them our neighbor.

19. Quote from a presentation given at PEER Servants' Ricchari Conference in Peru, August 2, 2007.

CHAPTER 2: MAKING A FEAST FOR JESUS

1. Special thanks to Keith Greer for his insights on the early Church, historical examples, and great reversal.

2. Rodney Stark, *The Rise of Christianity: A Sociologist Reconsiders History* (Princeton, NJ: Princeton University Press, 2006), 1.

3. J. Wesley Bready, *England: Before & After Wesley* (New York, NY: Harper & Brothers, 1940), 14.

4. Karen Swallow Prior, *Fierce Convictions: The Extraordinary Life of Hannah More: Poet, Reformer, Abolitionist* (Nashville, TN: Nelson Books, 2014). Special thanks to Chris Horst for his insights in this section.

5. Samuel Escobar and John Driver, *Introduction to Christian Mission & Social Justice* (Scottsdale, PA: Herald Press, 1978), 7–9.

6. Walter Rauschenbusch, *A Theology of the Social Gospel* (New York, NY: Macmillan, 1917), 145.

7. Bryant L. Myers, *Walking with the Poor* (New York, NY: Orbis, 2006), 6.

8. Mark Russell, "The Use of Business in Missions in Chiang Mai, Thailand," PhD dissertation (Wilmore, KY: Asbury Theological Seminary, 2008). This dissertation concerns missionaries who are involved in business as missions. In the dissertation, Russell contrasts two groups of missionaries. The first group says that their primary goal is to convert people to Christianity. The second group says that they are there to bless the people and to help them in numerous ways, such as finding meaningful employment, restoring relationships, providing for their families, etc. Which of these two groups is more effective in making disciples? Intuition might say the first group since they are not distracted by all the other things that the second group is trying to do. The finding was startling. The second group was more effective in making disciples by a 48-1 ratio.

9. David Kinnaman and Gabe Lyons, *UnChristian* (Grand Rapids, MI: Baker, 2007), 65.

10. Ibid., 70. The authors describe the Barna Group's research and how it relates to perceptions about Christians. When born-again Busters (their description) were asked how they came to faith, 71 percent responded that it was the result of a relationship.

CHAPTER 3: SEARCHING FOR SOLUTIONS THAT WORK

1. Jeff Rutt used this experience as the impetus to found HOPE International. Read his version of the story in the foreword.

2. This is not to insinuate that there are not benefits of short-term trips, particularly for the trip participants. Seth Barnes of Adventures in Missions describes that when people "step out of their comfort zones and embrace what God is doing around the world, they do not return the same." Well-orchestrated trips provide an opportunity to awaken men and women to their own brand of spiritual poverty and show them the difference that a living God at work in

their lives and in the lives of the people they meet can make to transform a community. He described some who go on trips as becoming "wrecked for the ordinary"—we celebrate when that is the case. But besides these positive impacts on the participants, we do need to simultaneously examine the impact on the recipients of our charity.

3. Joel Wickre, "Missions That Heal," *Christianity Today*, July 13, 2007, www.christianitytoday.com/ct/2007/julyweb-only/128-52.0.html.

4. Michael M. Phillips, "Unanswered Prayers: In Swaziland, US Preacher Sees His Dream Vanish," *Wall Street Journal*, December 19, 2005.

5. I am grateful to Roger Sandberg for his insightful articulation of these ideas at the 2010 Q Conference.

6. Giles Bolton, *Africa Doesn't Matter* (New York, NY: Arcade, 2008), 76.

7. Ibid., 224.

8. OECD, "Detailed aid statistics: Official and private flows," *OECD International Development Statistics* (database), 2016, DOI: dx.doi.org/10.1787/data-00072-en.

CHAPTER 4: A HAND UP, NOT A HANDOUT

1. Frank M. Loewenberg, *From Charity to Social Justice* (New Brunswick, NJ: Transaction, 2001), 95.

2. Marvin Olasky, *The Tragedy of American Compassion* (Washington, DC: Regnery, 1992), 9.

3. Ibid.

4. Ibid., 142.

5. Ibid., 154.

6. Steve Saint, *The Great Omission: Fulfilling Christ's Commission Completely* (Seattle, WA: YWAM, 2001), 102.

CHAPTER 5: UNLOCKING ENTREPRENEURSHIP

1. Nicholas Kristof, "You, Too, Can Be a Banker to the Poor," *The New York Times*, March 27, 2007.

2. Hernando de Soto, *The Mystery of Capital: Why Capitalism Triumphs in the West and Fails Everywhere Else* (New York, NY: Basic Books, 2000), 4.

3. Asli Demirguc-Kunt, Leora Klapper, Dorothe Singer, and Peter Van Oudheusden. *The Global Findex Database 2014: Measuring Financial Inclusion around*

ROMANIA

the World, Policy Research Working Paper 7255 (Washington, DC: World Bank, 2015), 4, datatopics. worldbank.org/financialinclusion.

4.   This story is adapted from one told by Stuart Rutherford in *The Poor and Their Money* (New Delhi, India: Oxford University Press, 2000), 13–20.

5.   On average, she has 550 rupees on deposit. 100/550 = 18 percent. Annualized, since she did this for only part of the year, it is 30 percent.

6.   "Flood survivors' savings washed away," *IRIN*, October 7, 2010, www.irinnews.org/feature/2010/10/07/flood-survivors-savings-washed-away.

7.   Ivan Murenzi, *Financial Inclusion in Rwanda 2016* (Kigali, Rwanda: Access to Finance Rwanda, 2016), 17, www.statistics.gov.rw/publication/finscope-rwanda-2016.

8.   Dave Larson, *MED Monday Minute*, Unpublished Newsletter, August 27, 2007.

9. Madeleine Bunting, "Bono Talks of US Crusade," *The Guardian*, June 16, 2005, www.guardian.co.uk/world/2005/jun/16/g8.usa.

10. "Children: reducing mortality," *World Health Organization*, January 2016, www.who.int/mediacentre/factsheets/fs178/en.

11. Opportunity International, "World Relief, World Relief Canada and Hope International Partner With Opportunity International to Open Microfinance Bank for Rwanda's Poor," August 7, 2007, www.prnewswire.com/news-releases/world-relief-world-relief-canada-and-hope-international-partner-with-opportunity-international-to-open-microfinance-bank-for-rwandas-poor-57935742.html.

CHAPTER 6: A BRASS RING

1. Stuart Rutherford, *The Poor and Their Money* (New Delhi, India: Oxford University Press, 2000), 41.

2. "Savings-Led Financial Services Working Group," *SEEP Network*, accessed August 17, 2016, www.seepnetwork.org/savings-led-financial-services-working-group-pages-10020.php.

3. Megan Gash and Kathleen Odell, *The Evidence-Based Story of Savings Groups: A Synthesis of Seven Randomized Control Trials* (Arlington, VA: The SEEP Network, 2013), 11, www.seepnetwork.org/filebin/pdf/resources/FINAL_Evidence-Based_Savings_Web.pdf.

CHAPTER 7: MICROFINANCE GOES MAINSTREAM

1. Srikant M. Datar, Marc J. Epstein, and Kristi Yuthas, "In Microfinance, Clients Must Come First," *Stanford Social Innovation Review*, Winter 2008, 44.

2. "Household Debt and Credit Report: Percent of Balance 90+ Days Delinquent," *Federal Reserve Bank of New York*, June 30, 2016, www.newyorkfed.org/microeconomics/hhdc.html.

3. Larry R. Reed, et al., "Mapping Pathways out of Poverty: The State of the Microcredit Summit Campaign Report, 2015," *Microcredit Summit Campaign*, November 11, 2015, stateofthecampaign.org/read-the-full-2015-report.

4. Inez Murray, "Catalyzing Women's Financial Inclusion: The Role of Data," *CGAP*, February 17, 2016, www.cgap.org/blog/catalyzing-women%E2%80%99s-financial-inclusion-role-data.

5. "UPS Gives $1 Million to Microlenders as Part of 100th Birthday Celebration," *Transport Topics*, November 12, 2007, 31.

CHAPTER 8: EXPLORING VARIATIONS

1. Larry R. Reed, et al., "Mapping Pathways out of Poverty: The State of the Microcredit Summit Campaign Report, 2015," *Microcredit Summit Campaign*, November 11, 2015, stateofthecampaign.org/read-the-full-2015-report.

2. Grameen Foundation, "Overcoming HIV and Building Her Community," accessed August 17, 2016, www.evancarmichael.com/African-Accounts/1678/Overcoming-HIV-and-Building-Her-Community.html.

3. "Active mobile telephone subscriptions as of May 2016," *Rwanda Utilities Regulatory Authority*, May 2016, www.rura.rw/fileadmin/docs/Monthly_telecom_subscribers_of__May__2016__1_.pdf.

4. Jessica C. Smith and Carla Medalia, *Health Insurance Coverage in the United States: 2014*, Current Population Reports P60-253 (Washington, DC: U.S. Census Bureau, 2015), 4, www.census.gov/content/dam/Census/library/publications/2015/demo/p60-253.pdf.

5. "About MicroEnsure," *MicroEnsure*, accessed August 18, 2016, microensure.com/about-microensure.

6. "Credit with Education," *Freedom from Hunger*, accessed August 18, 2016, www.freedomfromhunger.org/credit-education.

7. "About The HealthStore Foundation: Overview," *Child and Family Wellness Clinics*, accessed August 18, 2016, www.cfwshops.org/index.html.

8. M. K. Tally, "Job Training and Education Fight Poverty," Institute for Women's Policy Research Publication #D444, April 2002, www.iwpr.org/publications/pubs/job-training-and-education-fight-poverty.

9. "Undernutrition contributes to nearly half of all deaths in children under 5 and is widespread in Asia and Africa," *UNICEF Data*, June 2016, www.data.unicef.org/nutrition/malnutrition.html.

10. "Grameen Danone Foods Ltd," *Danone Communities*, accessed August 18, 2016, www.danonecommunities.com/en/project/grameen-danone-food?mode=history.

ROMANIA

11. CGAP and IFAD, *Emerging Lessons in Agricultural Microfinance: Selected Case Studies* (Rome, Italy: IFAD, 2006), 6, www.ifad.org/ruralfinance/pub/case_studies.pdf.

12. Muhammad Yunus, interview by NOW on PBS, *Enterprising Ideas*, accessed August 18, 2016, www.pbs.org/now/enterprisingideas/Muhammad-Yunus.html.

13. Muhammad Yunus, "Grameen Bank's Struggling (Beggar) Members Programme," *Yunus Centre*, July 2005, www.muhammadyunus.org/index.php/design-lab/previous-design-labs/43-news-a-media/books-a-articles/235-grameen-banks-struggling-beggar-members-programme.

14. Muhammad Yunus, interview by NOW on PBS, *Enterprising Ideas*, accessed August 18, 2016, www.pbs.org/now/enterprisingideas/Muhammad-Yunus.html.

15. Joanne Csete, *Policy Paralysis: A Call for Action on HIV/AIDS-Related Human Rights Abuses Against Women and Girls in Africa* (New York, NY: Human Rights Watch, 2003), 4, www.hrw.org/sites/default/files/reports/africa1203.pdf.

CHAPTER 9: IT CAN'T BE THAT GOOD, CAN IT?

1. Special thanks to Dave Larson for his contributions in this chapter.

2. Poverty Action Lab and Innovations for Poverty Action, "Where Credit Is Due," Policy Bulletin, February 2015, www.povertyactionlab.org/sites/default/files/publications/where-credit-is-due.pdf.

3. Muhammad Yunus, "Nobel Lecture," *Nobel Peace Prize 2006*, December 10, 2006, www.nobelprize.org/nobel_prizes/peace/laureates/2006/yunus-lecture-en.html.

4. Marcio Cruz, James Foster, Bryce Quillin, and Philip Schellekens, *Ending Extreme Poverty and Sharing Prosperity: Progress and Policies*, Policy Research Note (Washington, DC: World Bank, 2015), 6, pubdocs.worldbank.org/en/109701443800596288/PRN03Oct2015TwinGoals.pdf.

5. Anna Tibaijuka, "Report of the Fact-Finding Mission to Zimbabwe to assess the Scope and Impact of Operation Murambatsvina," *United Nations*, July 18, 2005, www.un.org/News/dh/infocus/zimbabwe/zimbabwe_rpt.pdf.

6. S. Shahzad Mustafa, "Anaphylaxis," *Medscape*, May 31, 2016, emedicine.medscape.com/article/135065-overview.

CHAPTER 10: USING THE SECOND-BEST DISTRIBUTION SYSTEM

1. Steve Corbett and Brian Fikkert, *When Helping Hurts: How to Alleviate Poverty Without Hurting the Poor … And Yourself* (Chicago: Moody Publishers, 2009), 22.

2. Warren Bird, "The World's Largest Churches: a country-by-country list of global megachurches," *Leadership Network*, accessed August 18, 2016, leadnet.org/world.

3. Junno Arocho Esteves, "Vatican statistics report increase in baptized Catholics worldwide," *National Catholic Reporter*, March 7, 2016, www.ncronline.org/news/vatican/vatican-statistics-report-increase-baptized-catholics-worldwide.

4. "Eastern Orthodoxy," *ReligionFacts*, November 10, 2015, www.religionfacts.com/eastern-orthodoxy.

5. "Our Mission and Vision," *Jobs for Life*, accessed August 18, 2016, www.jobsforlife.org/about.

CHAPTER 11: SAVING WITH THE CHURCH

1. Giles Bolton, *Africa Doesn't Matter: How the West Has Failed the Poorest Continent and What We Can Do about It* (New York, NY: Arcade, 2008), 289.

2. Kevin Tordoff, "The power of a new name," *HOPE International blog*, December 16, 2015, blog.hopeinternational.org/2015/12/16/the-power-of-a-new-name.

CHAPTER 13: PASTORS SELDOM MAKE GOOD BANKERS

1. Giles Bolton, *Africa Doesn't Matter: How the West Has Failed the Poorest Continent and What We Can Do about It* (New York, NY: Arcade, 2008), 140.

2. Tim Dearborn, "Living Our Christian Commitments, Remaining Faithful as a Christian Organization in a Changing World," Christian Commitments PowerPoint Presentation, World Vision International.

3. Paul Collier, *The Bottom Billion* (Oxford, England: Oxford University Press, 2007), 66.

4. Giles Bolton, *Africa Doesn't Matter: How the West Has Failed the Poorest Continent and What We Can Do about It* (New York, NY: Arcade, 2008), 88.

5. Ibid., 91.

CHAPTER 14: ROLLING UP OUR SLEEVES

1. Rick Warren, "On Mission: Pray For Specific Countries," *Pastor Rick's Daily Hope*, May 21, 2014, pastorrick.com/devotional/english/on-mission-pray-for-specific-countries.

2. Ronald Sider, *Rich Christians in an Age of Hunger* (Nashville, TN: Thomas Nelson, 2005), 28.

3. "Volunteer Profiles," *Peer Servants*, accessed August 18, 2016, www.peerservants.org/volunteer_profiles.html.

4. Greg Thompson. Personal Interview, December 15, 2008.

5. Abram Huyser Honig, "Study Questions Whether Short-Term Missions Make a Difference," *Christianity Today*, June 20, 2005, www.christianitytoday.com/ct/2005/juneweb-only/12.0c.html.

6. Peter Drucker, *The Practice of Management* (New York, NY: Harper & Brothers, 1954).

RWANDA

Photography Credits

Annie Rose Ansley (42, 117)

Isaac Barnes (12, 101, 156, 163)

Luke Boney (34, 75, 151, 206)

Jeff Brown (45, 91)

CCT (161)

Kelsey Fox (49, 79, 165, 245)

Peter Greer (37)

Drake Holtry (92, 203)

Alisa Hoober (198, 231)

Brady Kline (128, 220)

Nikole Lim (86, 107, 167)

Erin Longenecker (115, 185, 235)

Joanne Lu (71, 147, 227)

Chris McCurdy (177)

Shami Mugisha (137)

Tyson Presnell (64, 125)

Jennifer Priddy (inside front cover)

Michael Rothermel (30, 119, 131, 144, 200, 243, inside back cover)

Hanna Ruth (197)

Sarah Severns (76, 122, 195, 211)

Alexia Skoriak (82, 141, 238, 240)

Phil Spreadbury (back cover)

Matt Stockamp (60, 68, 103, 134, 170, 209, 222)

Rebecca Svendsen (cover, 94, 155, 180, 190, 216)

Sarah Tan (53)

Stephanie Walker (112)

Annalise Wood (158)

BOOKS BY PETER GREER

The Giver and the Gift
(coauthored by David Weekley)

40/40 Vision
(coauthored by Greg Lafferty)

Mission Drift
(coauthored by Chris Horst with Anna Haggard)

The Spiritual Danger of Doing Good
(with Anna Haggard)

Entrepreneurship for Human Flourishing
(coauthored by Chris Horst)

Watching Seeds Grow
(coauthored by Keith Greer)

Mommy's Heart Went Pop!
(coauthored by Christina Kyllonen)

Created to Flourish
(coauthored by Phil Smith)

BOOKS BY PHIL SMITH

A Billion Bootstraps
(coauthored by Eric Thurman)

Created to Flourish
(coauthored by Peter Greer)

HOPE
INTERNATIONAL

About HOPE International

HOPE International invests in the dreams of families in the world's underserved communities as we proclaim and live the Gospel. We provide discipleship, biblically based training, savings services, and small loans, empowering women and men to use the skills God has placed in their hands to provide for their families and strengthen their communities.

For specific resources on HOPE International's approach to spiritual integration, operations, fundraising, and more, visit our online resource portal at *www.hopeinternational.org/resources.*

www.hopeinternational.org